JOE'S STORY

"A compelling, poignant telling of a remarkable life."
— Tim Russert —
NBC's *Meet the Press*

"The life and death of a great soul, told with love and honesty."
— Tom Fontana —
Television writer and producer
("OZ," "Judas," "The Jury," "Homicide," "St. Elsewhere")

"Joe Bissonette didn't only live it,
but pushed the envelope on brotherly love."
— Honorable John T. Curtin —
U.S. District Court Judge

"I have just finished your book and am absolutely stunned
by the complete history and your writing of it.
Up to now, I was aware of very little."
— Mark Russell —
Political Satirist

"If I ever met a saint, it was Joe Bissonette.
This book is a powerful confirmation of that recollection."
— Honorable Edgar NeMoyer —
New York State Court of Claims Justice (retired)
and former college classmate of Joe's.

Publisher: A. Joseph Bissonette Memorial Foundation
Book Design: Mary Lu Littlefield

Printed in the United States of America
by digital @batesjackson llc
(716) 854-3000
Library of Congress Catalog Number Pending
ISBN 1-932583-16-5

JOE'S STORY

The quietly courageous life and violent death of an inner city priest.

RAY BISSONETTE

DEDICATION

My mother and father, two seemingly ordinary people, who fashioned an extraordinary son, merit much of the credit for the story. My wife, Ann, whose love for Joe drew him more closely into our lives, enriched his life and later made the Memorial Foundation a success. In 2004, Bill Stanton died. His admiration for Joe and tireless contributions to the work of the Foundation are unrivalled. The influence of these people on Joe was powerful and profound, but sadly, their testimony is mute and implicit. Finally, among those who can't speak, is Joe, for whom my love and respect has grown immensely through this effort. How little I knew, how little I knew. For half a century, someone who seemed so close, I saw only "through a glass darkly."

CONTENTS

ACKNOWLEDGMENTS

The Trustees of the Bissonette Foundation, who, some years ago in an almost unanimous vote, elected me as biographer, started the project. Dozens of others, through direct or indirect testimony gave it substance. Careful reading in the draft stages by Joanne Lucas, Evelyn McLean Brady, Grace Febres, and Sister Jeremy Midura, brought distant memories into sharp focus. The final steps, far more involved than I ever imagined, were managed with the help of many more. Professor Joe Bieron showed me the mechanics. Mary Lu Littlefield, who edited, designed, formatted, and generally brought this to completion, has been invaluable. George Schaeffer's graphic wizardry provided extensive material for the cover design. Copy editing by Lisa Murray-Roselli, Virginia O'Brien Lohr and Pat Donlon was critical fine-tuning. Misjudgments, factual errors, glitches in the text, and other lapses, belong to me.

Ray Bissonette, January 2005

FOREWORD

Ray Bissonette's superbly written Buffalo-based odyssey of Rev. Joseph Bissonette, the "priests' priest" of the poor and the marginal, could be a reminder that the Catholic Church is not alas, a wing of the Republican party.

Ray's brother Joe was one of the good ones — a priest whose life refutes the cynical notion that Jesus was not only the first Christian but the last. Father Bissonette's Calvary came on a horrifying night of ghastly tragedy when he was making sandwiches for two street punks who knocked on his door and said they were hungry. Then they stabbed him to death.

With humor and a total disregard for money — other than giving it to others, Bissonette marched and demonstrated while taking up the causes of the disenfranchised — be they in the down-at-the-heels neighborhoods of Buffalo, Birmingham or Managua. His reward was often a sneer of disapproval from the Your Excellencies on high.

Joe Bissonette's was a life of faith, skimpy meals, crummy living quarters and, for a time, a dim bishop for a boss. The story is told against the backdrop of late 20th Century events which ignited Joe's conscience and because he is no longer with us — too many of the comforted in Buffalo and elsewhere are going unafflicted.

Of the three traditional priestly vows, Father Bissonette handled the poverty and the chastity, but had a bit of a problem with the obedience. For that we can be grateful, for it is written (by me, I guess): Blessed are the troublemakers, for they shall drive the hierarchy crazy.

Mark Russell,
Political Satirist

PREFACE

"Seek not the favor of the multitude; it is seldom got by honest and lawful means. But seek the testimony of the few; and number not the voices, but weigh them." — Immanuel Kant

This admonition comes as close as anything I've seen to a distillation of what Joe believed and how he lived. The story that unfolds here will appear, albeit fortuitously, as having taken its cue from that advice. Fifteen years after Joe's death and two centuries after Kant's, these thoughts were echoed in a Lenten reflection read at Mass in March 2002 by Evelyn Brady, who had known Joe only briefly.

> At this time of year, when we celebrate the fifteenth anniversary of Joe Bissonette's tragic death, Jesus' words hold special meaning: 'everyone who exalts himself shall be humbled and he who humbles himself shall be exalted.' With his extraordinary intelligence, gifted people-skills, his passionate dedication, Joe could have been 'exalted' as a doctor, a senator, even a bishop. He was a leader. And yet we didn't 'follow' Joe; we were attracted to the fullness of the Spirit in him. Joe lived Jesus' message. Do you remember how Joe treated each person, whether a drug addict on the street, or one of us, as if there would never again be anyone as wondrous? Do you remember how he never took his priestly role as a superior station, but as way to serve, to be one of us? Do you remember how he would not judge our indi-

> vidual human flaws, but used his energy to publicly protest structural injustices? Do you remember how he identified with the poor in a way that gave them pride? Joe put aside his ambitions for self-promotion for one purpose: to be freer to love. Joe humbled himself so we would feel our worth. Today, fifteen years later, we can exalt Joe for he taught us how to live in humility. We can understand this passage because of Joe Bissonette. Our challenge is no less.

This memoir, will validate those words of Immanuel and Evelyn, not by design but by the weight of evidence, as nearly as that can be adduced from a personal recollection that draws from my memory, that of others close to Joe, and various sources such as books, periodicals, and the media. The story emerging from that totality is less likely to be skewed by the bias of any single source, yet the bulk of the tale is what was seen through my eyes and recalled from my memory. Accordingly, you will not find here anything purporting to be pure objectivity, only an honest effort to be true to the history of someone who valued the truth more than most. What to call this is another question. Typically, biographies are formal, comprehensive, and presented as objective. This work, in its relative informality, reliance on my recall, and selection and synthesis of material, tips toward memoir. For most readers, what will be key is accuracy and honesty. I have been scrupulous about this, albeit cognizant of the inherent problems in any such work. What is here, while not exhaustive, is at least, to the best of my ability, true. Kathryn Harrison, a modern novelist and herself the author of a memoir, puts the problem of objectivity in such an enterprise very well:

"Narrative is made from the rubble of experience, a necessarily retrospective process of assembling those details that contribute to the chosen story, discarding others, equally true, that might resolve into another picture." Another cautionary note was sounded by the far better known, Virginia Woolf: "Each has his past shut in him like the leaves of a book known to him by heart and his friends can only read the title." This, picture, then, while not the perfect picture is the only one of its kind; soon to be the only one at all. *Caveat lector.*

CHAPTER ONE

CAPTAIN AMERICA

Leaping exuberantly from bed to bed, brandishing a yardstick and trailing one of the sheets as his cape, Captain America, then in the person of nine-year old Joe Bissonette, would leave my sister and me squealing in excitement. Within that house we rented at 37 Shirley Avenue in Buffalo, NY, were my earliest memories of Joe. My knowledge of the Captain, a comic book hero who first appeared in 1941, was only through Joe's rendering of the role. I was between two and three and my sister, Joanne, seven. Soon after, we left Shirley Avenue and the Captain behind, never guessing that Joe would wear a cape as an adult and continue to be Captain America for others who needed a champion for very different reasons.

Another vivid memory, adding some balance to the happy scenes of Captain America and his adoring sibs, took place also on Shirley Avenue during a winter backyard marshmallow roast over a fire in a steel drum. Joanne was cooking with a meat fork and got into some kind of argument with Joe. Suddenly she threw the fork at him and I watched, as though in slow motion it flipped end over end and stuck quivering in his leg. Horrified, Joanne ran in the house screaming hysterically, and then threw up. Joe appeared mainly surprised then unhappy when the iodine was applied. Other memories of Joe in those days were mostly of my frustration and tears when he went off with the "big guys," John Zeitler, Frank Stickel, Gibby Stengel, Dave Pasiak, and others, while I whined about being left behind, although often they would include me in the softball games played in the field at the end of the street. I got to chase the balls the fielders missed.

Our days on Shirley Avenue, which ended around my fifth and Joe's twelfth year, also marked my first awareness of a ubiquitous evil that would stalk children and parents for many years to come. One summer day as I stood on the front walk in my underwear enjoying a warm rain shower, a large vehicle swung into the driveway across the street. I stood transfixed, never having seen such a machine. It was an ambulance that left with my friend Jimmy Tschopp. He waved to me and never came home. He died of polio.

The Second World War was raging during those days, and even as children we were keenly aware of the constant reminders of a country mobilizing to support and later join the allies: the radio announcements imploring young men to enlist ("We need manpower"); the rationing; the olive drab aircraft to which we waved frantically; the victory gardens; and the air raid drills when my mother would let us get out of bed to sit in the darkened living room listening to the sirens. My father wouldn't be there; he had left earlier with his special air raid warden helmet, rushing off in his car to participate in some kind of emergency drill.

We had at least two relatives in the war: a cousin, Franny Bissonette, and my mother's younger brother, Ed Sharkey, who survived the Normandy beaches on D-day only to sustain a lasting injury in a motorcycle accident while a patrolman for the Lockport police.

For the most part, the war was to me, and probably to Joe and Joanne, distant in space and impact. Most of what we experienced directly were, to us, novelties. And many other harsh realities of those days of simple distinctions between black and white hats were unknown, not only to children but to nearly everyone. The knowledge that much of our local industry was preparing not only aircraft engines but components of Little Boy and Fat Man would be buried with its toxic byproducts for decades.

Absent as well from our awareness were the dark realities of power, later to be known as Realpolitik, that would intersect with Joe's life as he later chose to question the role of our own leadership in implementing oppression and persecution.

Sister Joanne at age 3 with Joe, age 5

CHAPTER TWO

WHY CAN'T YOU BE LIKE YOUR BROTHER?

Joe was seven years my senior and my sister, Joanne, five. Throughout my childhood I trailed them both in years and the impression made on the adult world. Both preceded me through Buffalo Public School 63 where they stood out as popular and accomplished, respected by peers and teachers. In those days (the 1940s) an award called the Jesse Ketchum medal was given to the seventh and eighth graders with the highest academic average. Joanne won it in eighth grade and Joe won it twice. (I am told this recollection is faulty — the medal was only awarded in the eighth grade; but correct or not it sticks in my mind. Maybe because Joe was such a towering figure to me, something that extraordinary just had to be true.) To me it was close to miraculous and certainly far out of reach. I was not academically handicapped but lacked the discipline to go that extra mile. I probably didn't realize it then but learned soon enough that the discipline issue was to be what set me apart from both of the giant killers ahead of me. Frustrated and angry teachers would often ask why I couldn't be like my brother and sister. To me that was just a silly question — they were a different species. But the question carried a sting when it came from Barts, the gym teacher and principal arbiter of status in that preadolescent and pre-political correctness world.

Joe made the teams and continued to throughout high school and college. He was a respected athlete but would always be limited by lacking the Vince Lombardi view of competition and victory. Many years later I was reminded of this when he and I played squash at the Canisius College Athletic Center. As his lead began to build I'd notice the serves coming slower and softer. It annoyed me but I knew he would rather lose than hurt my feelings. That sensitivity explained a lot about how he lived and why he died.

Among the memorabilia of Joe that my mother kept in her dresser after his death (all the pictures and plaques had been turned face down) was a black and white snapshot enlarged to an eight by ten. It shows Joe in mid-air, just releasing a jump shot. It has no labeling but was quite clearly taken in the gym at St. Joseph's School, probably during a CYC (Catholic Youth Council, later Catholic Youth Organization) game in his late high school or early college years. It's a powerful reminder of a special trait of his that I, and most who knew him as a young man, remember well. He loved sports and competed well, but felt no need to dance on anyone's chest. For some, that represented a shortcoming sure to hold him back, and perhaps it was. But I know of no one whose respect for him was in any way diminished by that failing.

While he may have lacked the killer instinct, he was sufficiently competitive to earn his place on the field and, in fact, once advised me gently after watching me play CYC basketball that I needed to be more aggressive. Joe Brown, who often played with and against Joe in CYC games and pick-up games at school playgrounds, reminded me several times that Joe "had sharp elbows." Clearly he was aggressive enough even if he didn't fight, and maybe that was why he didn't. But Joe's sharp elbows, as his lifelong friend John Zeitler would explain years later, had a different quality if not a different feel. As John, a legendary athlete in Buffalo, who later played professional baseball, put it, "...when Joe used his elbows, he thought about it, for other guys it was just natural."

He grew tall early, worked at staying in shape and continued to throughout his life. He competed well, often excelled, and wasn't a wiseguy. He never seemed to be in the scrapes that were chronic in my younger years. Maybe he didn't fight because he didn't have to prove himself. In any case, my father misread the signs if he confused Joe's lack of physical aggressiveness with insufficient courage to make his way in the world. Joe's courage was much deeper and would prove to have commensurate consequences, one of them fatal.

And while Joe was in high school, people far away and totally unknown to him or any of us were generating change that would intersect with Joe's life years later. In the post war years, William Levitt was perfecting the mass-produced single family home to draw thousands of returning GIs to Levittown and similar suburban developments throughout the country. As that phenomenon coincided with the huge migrations of blacks from the rural south to the northern industrial inner cities, the stage was being set for the impoverished minority-populated inner city communities, in one of which Joe would find a career and meet his death.

Another man was reaching the zenith of his career at General Motors. Harley Earl, the tsar of design in the world's largest corporation, had created a corporate culture where form dictated function and engineering took a back seat to style. The era of planned obsolescence in consumer products had become the norm. This would have global economic and social consequences, but for Joe it was one of many developments that would contribute to his suspicion of the corporate world. How often I remember hearing him curse "those bastards" who deliberately designed products intended to last only for the short term. Of course this would affect Joe very directly throughout his life, due to his habit of driving cars whose useful life was over long before he owned them.

CHAPTER THREE

MAYBE HE'LL BE A PRIEST

My father grew up as the oldest of seven and became head of the family early as his father's alcoholism progressed. In his boyhood, disputes were settled with fists. He always worried about Joe because he wouldn't fight. For my father, this was a serious handicap in a young man facing a tough world. The boxing gloves and lessons in the basement didn't change a thing. "Come on, hit me," Dad would urge, but Joe's swings were half hearted. My mother told us many years later that my father had wished Joe would become a priest. In those days, among Catholics, that was a high aspiration and clearly well suited to someone with Joe's intellectual bent and apparent lack of aggressiveness. No one in the family ever seriously expected that to happen, including my father who never lived to see it. He died when Joe was still in Canisius College, but lived long enough to witness Joe's athletic accomplishments and the beginnings of even greater success in an environment where toughness was measured in terms other than physical. A former colleague of Joe's, during her time in the religious life, penned a poem that articulated and expanded my father's prescient apprehension about Joe's fit in a tough world. The verse, by Dorothy Smith, introduced a workbook on social justice released in 1998 by Timothy Alan and Elizabeth Goodine.

Some thoughts about Joe
as told by mother
this child Joe.
too good for a not so good world
mother and father
thank God
Joe chose the priesthood

Only thing is
Joe thought the priesthood was real
more real than the dark
Joe believed he could, he should
heal, cure, comfort, teach
reach with a gentleness, even humor
into the darkest nights
where the priesthood led him
did he reach too far
did he understand his world

his priesthood too little
or too much
that he set out so soon
for Jerusalem

My father's aspirations were not without basis. Early in life Joe displayed a noticeable piety that seemed generally recognized and accepted among those who knew him. One incident that captures that quality for me occurred one Good Friday at St. Joseph's Church in north Buffalo, our parish for many years. While making my obligatory visit, I ran into Jim Cullen, a neighbor and friend of Joe's for many years. Assuming that he and Joe were together, I asked him where Joe was. He shrugged in resignation and replied, "He's going around a third time." What he referred to was the "stations of the cross," a devotional practice in which Christ's crucifixion was remembered by performing a prescribed set of prayers and meditations at each of fourteen representations lining the sidewalls of Catholic churches. It was a lengthy and, for me, tedious practice that you would do only on Good Friday. But you always felt good when you finished; and for me and most kids it was mainly because you had finished. A second round was above and beyond — a third was unheard of.

In hindsight, Joe's seeming disinclination for physical violence may have only been partly inherent. Several incidents suggest that it, like his celibacy, were the products of choice and plain determination. A few years after Joe's death, I met Jack O'Connor, an official in the County Department of Social Services who had been a student of Joe's at Turner High School, fought in Viet Nam, and returned to settle in Buffalo. We were talking about the murder and his first question was, "How did they get the drop on him?" I reminded him that there were two of them and a knife. He remained skeptical and I asked him why. He then told me of playing basketball against Joe during the faculty-student games at Turner and once, under the boards, calling Joe a son of a bitch. Joe chased him the length of the court where he caught him, lifted him off the floor till they were eye to eye, and asked him to repeat what he'd said. His recollection of this was so vivid that he could not imagine that only two men and one knife could have prevailed against the priest he remembered.

There were other isolated but similar incidents. One of these Joe related to me many years ago and apparently told to no one else. He had been somewhere out of town at a conference or perhaps working on his master's in Religious Education when he visited a local public beach. While there he watched a group of young men amusing themselves at the waterfront by tossing passing females into the water. He grew increasingly angry and finally walked down and invited them to throw him in. They declined. Perhaps the most significant of these incidents for Joe was the housebreaker and the fireplace poker. Early in his assignment to St. Bartholomew's he was up in his room one night when he heard noises from the first floor. While investigating he discovered a pair of hands outside the pantry removing shards of glass from the newly broken window. It was obvious that someone was making his way into the house. Joe went first to the phone to call the police then to the fireplace; returning to the pantry with the poker and waiting for the intruder to make his entrance. The police arrived before the poker was needed, but that was not the end of the story. By then, Joe's commitment to non-violence was taking clear shape and the knowledge that he had prepared himself to use a potential deadly weapon on someone worried him greatly. I knew nothing of that at the time, but a year after his death at a dinner for the Sisters of Social Service where Joe was honored posthumously, the head of the local community recalled how Joe had wrestled with the memory of his intent and capacity to use violence during that night of the break-in attempt. The details from the night of his murder will offer intriguing insights on Jack O'Connor's question of how they "...got the drop on him."

The so-called "five sticks of dynamite" of Canisius High School Varsity Basketball. Joe is at center top of photo.

**St. Joseph Church Muni Baseball League 1948.
Joe in second from right in top row.**

CHAPTER FOUR

THE EVIL OF FOLDING CORNERS

After high school, my father had joined a religious order known as the Passionist Fathers. This vocation was short lived as deteriorating conditions at home forced him to return and find a job. As the oldest male in a family of seven children, it fell to him to keep the family intact. My mother had studied art at the Albright School and taught for several years but, once married, seemed content to devote herself to the family. My father, however, was frustrated by many thwarted dreams and a job as an insurance salesman that was not only stressful but reminded him constantly of being locked in by lack of higher education and an economy that, for many, effectively foreclosed letting go of whatever you had that would pay the bills.

Doubtless, this situation accounted for the value placed on education in our family. For them and most Americans of modest means, it was the one and only path to a better life for their children. One consequence of this was Joe's enrollment at Canisius High School, a Jesuit school regarded as one of the best high schools in the city, but available at a cost requiring significant sacrifice in our house. But Joe, and Joanne, who attended Sacred Heart Academy, would reward that sacrifice as later I might also, but my father lived only long enough to learn that I did *not* win the Jesse Ketchum medal in eighth grade.

Many of Joe's habits, good and bad, could be explained by his being the first born in a family started during a period when fully one quarter of the population was unemployed. Joe was doubtless impressed by some of the broader societal forces that impinged on most families in that time, to say nothing of our own. One did not waste anything, including time, and learning was the key to the opportunities so many in the preceding generation had missed.

For Joe, the key became an end in itself. He revered learning and all its accouterments. His later course of life revealed clearly a search for continuous upgrading of his knowledge. He rarely missed an opportunity for an educational experience, but his motives seemed consistent with learning for its own sake rather than for any status it might confer. For all the time and energy he committed to study, he never seemed inclined to gain a terminal degree. He completed numerous workshops and master's degrees, all of which tended to be relatively invisible. Even many of his close friends were unaware that he completed three master's degrees beyond his college and seminary training. From Canisius College he received an M.A. in history in 1963; from Loyola University in Chicago, a master of religious education degree in 1970; and from Christ the King Seminary, a master of divinity degree in 1975. In anticipation of an inner city ministry, he even completed a workshop in Afro-American music in Indiana. In retrospect, it's not surprising that he viewed books as treasures. You did not mark your place by bending corners of pages — a bit of information I picked up when he caught me doing it. Books were sacred. He treated them as though each volume had been hand-copied in an Irish monastery. Bending page corners was not only destructive of a precious possession but disrespectful.

His near devotion to reading was evident not only in the words of an early pastor puzzled by Joe's ceaseless reading but appears again in his diary from a ten-week internship he took with Congressman John LaFalce in the fall of 1979. His recreational reading included novels by Malamud, Bellow, Cheever, Uris, Irving, Vonnegut, and Updike. In all, he read and commented on eight books in ten weeks including *Trinity* that, by most people's reckoning, would count for a couple. He was completing nearly a novel a week while working long days, devouring Washington, D.C., keeping current on newspapers and periodicals, managing his priestly role, and visiting friends almost every weekend. This discipline and energy may have explained the comments by nearly everyone interviewed for this memoir that Joe was "always there," and the avid and broad reading was a life long pattern that both contributed to and reflected his generally liberal views as a person and priest. Poetry was not his first choice in literature, but I am reminded by my sister that he had a lifelong love for Robert Frost.

Other books Joe surely remembered better than I were the wartime gas rationing coupon books and the huge ledger in which my father recorded the twenty-five and fifty cent weekly premiums he collected from his life insurance customers — the means by which he struggled to support our family during Joe's childhood during the Great Depression, in the trough of which Joe was born.

CHAPTER FIVE

INTEGRITY

After Joe's death, I was called on many times to speak on behalf of our family, usually at events where he was being honored posthumously. My principal theme, which I believed best captured what Joe's life was about, was integrity. I took it in its most fundamental sense — unity; that in Joe's case was the essential integration of thought, word, and deed. It sounds almost Pollyanna-ish and a bit preachy; still I have never had reason to doubt its basic truth in characterizing Joe. And I don't know when or how it began. It seems always to have been there, although certain memories stand out.

When Joe was a teenager, our family vacationed for a week or two each summer at a semi-working farm in Wyoming County where, as they grew older, Joe and Joanne worked off their lodging costs. It was a magical place for all of us but I went only once for two weeks. While there I learned something about Joe's sense of fairness that would inform many of his life choices. For me the story was so telling that I used it in my remarks at the first anniversary commemoration of his death. I was eight years old and Joe fourteen. Another guest, Roe Judd, from somewhere downstate, was two years my senior. From the moment of my arrival, the dance of dominance began with Roe leading. One afternoon he and I were playing with squirt guns behind the farmhouse. Suddenly, his tormenting drove me beyond my fear and I picked up a galvanized water bucket to dump on him. To my surprise he ran and I went after him until he tripped in the ditch beside the dirt road leading to the barn.

I jumped or fell on top of him and began pummeling wildly. It was a gratifying moment for me as my pent-up anger took over and his shrieks signaled a new dance. But then, above the sound of Roe's wailing, I heard the clanking of harnesses as the hay wagon approached the barn and pulled up abruptly above us. Looking up, I could see all the young teen-aged gods, hayforks in hand, tanned, sweaty, and stripped to the waist. And I heard the comments about the fact that I was hammering Roe with a bucket. Then Joe, from whom I expected reproach, simply said, " Roe's bigger and older." The discussion was over. I learned that sometimes the underdog needs a little special advantage to even things up, and Joe would spend much of his life trying to put buckets where they were needed.

Joe's high school years, 1946-1950, were during the post-war period of relative prosperity and apparent simplicity. It was an interlude during which young people could look forward to a safer, more predictable world. The mythic 1950s were in the making. The nation was dancing to Guy Lombardo and Sammy Kaye, singing about a "Slow Boat to China," and watching Broderick Crawford portray the Kingfish in *All the King's Men.* Norma Jean Baker changed her name to Marilyn Monroe, and Albert Kinsey turned his attention from gall wasps to sex to reveal the vast chasm between the mores portrayed by the Aldrich family and the actual sexual behavior of Americans. The Dow broke 225 and "Goodnight Irene" topped the hit parade, but at Canisius High School, the favorite song was "Stardust," and Joe Bissonette's highest ambition was reported to be "to have a date." Perhaps more important was the possible adumbration of his life-long honesty contained in his senior yearbook. Under the heading of "favorite expressions," Joe is quoted as saying "I didn't do the homework, Father."

But the post war years leading to the fabled simplicity and stability of the 1950s were as far from our nostalgic memories as sexual standards were from the behavior unearthed by Kinsey's extensive investigation. The Russian bear was prowling the earth, exhibiting awesome versatility in extending its turf through stealth, brute force, or whatever worked. Late in the decade, the Soviets exploded a nuclear bomb and a half-century of Cold War began. Eruptions of open but limited warfare would mark the entire period. Korea was the most dramatic, but oppression and bloodshed were ubiquitous and Joe's mother would remark to him one afternoon that, instead of history and literature, he might have to learn to use a howitzer. On May 8, 1954, only days before Joe's graduation from Canisius College, the French stronghold at Dien Bien Phu in northern Viet Nam fell after months of savage battle with the Viet Minh under rebel leader Ho Chi Minh. Ending French colonial rule in Indochina, the defeat divided the country into the communist north and the western-allied south, setting the stage for American military involvement that would result in a second ignominious defeat for a western power and a redefinition of the political and moral landscape of the United States. In a tiny country across the globe, a lengthy war of attrition fed the growth of a generation of Americans who distrusted and defied official leadership and directly or indirectly set the stage for a critical minority committed to peace and non-violence. Joe would soon take his place among them.

Political sidebars were significant and tumultuous. A young Congressman named Richard Nixon was building a political career by rooting out communist spies and sympathizers from our government, and the House Committee on Un-American Activities was rolling our hard-won system of civil liberties back to the days of the Inquisition. Soon, another politician, Senator Joseph McCarthy, would find anti-communism the basis for a major political power play. Curiously, McCarthy's short but long-remembered career as demagogue of the decade began almost by accident. Speaking at a 1950 Lincoln Day celebration of the Ohio County Women's Republican Club in Wheeling, West Virginia, the Republican Senator from Wisconsin mentioned, almost as an aside, that he had in his pocket a list of communists serving in the U.S. government. There was no such list, but the intense interest of the press and the obvious political leverage of leading the parade of politicians seeking to regain government control from the Democrats, moved him to ferret out potential suspects. And ferret he did until his own political and alcoholic excesses brought him down years later.

But the soil was tilled for a generation of fear, real or imagined, of communism's spread throughout the planet. Those fears, entrenched in American consciousness and policy would, decades later, collide with Joe's spiritual quest for a just world where oppression could not be tolerated because it allegedly contained the advance of communism. For him, these contradictions were most troubling in Central America where he saw the United States vigorously supporting ruthless dictatorships, so long as they were opposed to communism. In 1953, riding high on his college popularity and struggling with his decision about the priesthood, Joe would have been, along with most Americans, unaware of the roots of the Latin American policies that would later enrage him and, ironically, place two Central American refugees in his house the night he was killed. But that year, in Iran, an upstart prime minister had the temerity to threaten western oil interests and display a left-leaning political stance that worried the United States in those early Cold War years when the Soviet Union was flexing its muscle around the globe. The U.S. and Britain collaborated in a coup that replaced the Prime Minister, Mossadegh, with Shah Pahlevi without a drop of blood spilled. Encouraged by its first big and easy win in the Cold War, the CIA next turned its attention to Guatemala, where another presumably Soviet-influenced leader was interfering with the autonomy of the United Fruit Company. To me, and most casual consumers of news about American foreign affairs, this was just another laudable effort in the battle against the spreading evil of communism. And that uncritical acceptance for most of us would and does continue, so that Joe's outrage later in the 1970s and 1980s seemed extreme, and possibly the consequence of naïve zealotry. Sadly, Joe never lived to see his convictions vindicated with the release in the 1990s of State Department records confirming our active support of brutally oppressive policies in Central America, especially El Salvador.

When Joe was a young priest in the 1970s, some of the consequences of oppression in Central America were hitting our shores. The response to this among peace activists in Buffalo was formation of a group called the Medical Aid to El Salvador Committee that was established to assist both the Central American residents and refugees who were beginning to arrive in large numbers. The influx of refugees triggered another initiative. Usually en route to Canada, a process that required temporary residence in the United States after an initial appearance at Canadian immigration, refugees needed substantial help with housing, legal issues, and social support. As a border city, Buffalo was a major point of entry and site of the temporary stays while awaiting clearance for entry into Canada. The Buffalo facility to meet this need, VIVE La Casa, now located in a former school on Buffalo's east side, was born in those years. Initially, the housing was provided by a parish in Lackawanna augmented by the hospitality of individual families and church rectories. Joe provided leadership for both programs that continue to this day. But before formal services were in place and fully operational, Joe was among a number of religious and laypersons who offered asylum to refugees. During the 1980s, he regularly hosted refugees while pastor at St. Bartholomew's. Ironically, the two staying on his third floor in February 1987 would, for a time, become suspects in his murder. At the first anniversary of his death, one of the laypersons working with him on aid to El Salvador, Bridget Murphy, spoke at the memorial in St. Joseph's Church recalling these years of the covert asylum movement and Joe's leadership in it. Among her recollections were two seemingly divergent images of Joe: his arrival at the Medical Aid to El Salvador dinner early and departure late, after he had helped prepare the meal and stayed to clean up; and later, his homilies at the Archbishop Romero Mass, during one of which he spoke of being ashamed of his government for its mistreatment of Latin American poor in the name of halting communism. The easy coexistence in Joe of leader and servant was his hallmark and reminds one of his "mentor" who washed the feet of the poor one day and preached to the multitudes another.

Despite the excesses of our government's response, the threat from communism was real enough, and Joe would live and die in a world dominated by the specter of nuclear holocaust and atrocities of various magnitudes arising from the struggle between the democratic and communist ideology, plus many other injustices resulting from self serving behavior having nothing to do with ideology. Ironically, later in life he would often find himself leaning far to the left, as he saw the deification of free enterprise create vast concentrations of wealth and power among the few, leaving many with only leftovers and worse if they complained.

During Joe's youth, America, while always officially and often, in fact, standing against opponents of individual liberty, was a society of widely institutionalized racism. Segregation was a reality everywhere and remained so in practice and policy throughout most of the South well into the 1950s and later. That this era bred thousands of idealistic young people committed to social justice is no surprise. That Joe Bissonette, who always followed the rules, emerged from his formative years in this environment alienated from officialdom even in the Church where he sought integrity and justice is also no surprise.

CHAPTER SIX

COMING OF AGE

The 1950s, despite their vast inequities and political divisiveness, were widely depicted as a period of an orderly peaceful post war American society where family, community, and Church were dominant values. They were also Joe's formative years.

The beginning of the baby boom, coupled with the arrival of mass communication through television, contributed to the images believed by many to this day of white picket fences surrounding households of stable, wholesome family units doing their part for and sharing in the American dream. History shows a different reality; even then, disturbing messages were emerging in academia and popular culture, raising questions about the vaunted world of Ozzie and Harriet. Grace Metalius's *Peyton Place*, Vladimir Nobokov's *Lolita*, and John O'Hara's novels gave dramatic fictional color to Kinsey's evidence of sharp discrepancies between actual and professed behaviors behind the picket fences and ruffled curtains. And serious students of society revealed deep fault lines in the orderly workings of capitalism as the ideal vehicle for personal and social development. The voices of David Riesman, Vance Packard, William H. Whyte, and others told of corrosive forces inherent in the system we so badly needed to believe would finally deliver us from warfare and insecurity to peace, tranquility, and prosperity. And at the Supreme Court on May 17, 1954, the *Brown vs. the Board of Education* decision buried the convenient separate but equal rationale for school desegregation, providing at once a leap forward in the civil rights movement and a dark picture of the tenacity of racism a century after the Civil War. The legal ruling of nine gray eminences didn't uproot deep, virulent hatreds.

In August of the year following the Court decision, Emmet Till, a 14 year-old black boy from Chicago, was visiting his aunt and uncle in Money, Mississippi. Allegedly, he whistled at a white woman; and his mutilated body was later found in the Tala-hatchie River. His killers were acquitted and later boasted in *Look* magazine of how and why they taught him a lesson. The fury of their assault would be matched years later in two Buffalo church rectories, when two black boys not much older than Emmett would vent their rage on a white priest in their world. In this age of sharp contradictions and smoldering emotions, one of those victims would come of age.

But the social and economic forces that would create the conditions and neighborhoods to which Joe would direct his ministry were churning long before the Supreme Court dismissed the concept of separate but equal and demanded public school integration. Massive assembly line manufacturing and labor intensive industry in the North, fired by two world wars, were drawing thousands of southern blacks to the urban industrial centers. Buffalo was among them. Immigrant groups from the nineteenth century were first joined then displaced by the southern migrants as the inner cities were being vacated by the whites who bought the newly available suburban homes financed by GI loans and easily accessed in mass-produced, affordable automobiles.

Liberal financing opportunities, virtually unavailable in the cities for blacks, facilitated the white flight. Left behind were urban areas of old housing stock, affordable by the latest arrivals — low skill, low-income southern blacks. And then the mills and factories closed up, leaving a human residue of minorities, mainly black, locked into chronic poverty that, for many, became a way of life. Left behind too, were the grand places of worship built in every neighborhood by the Irish, Italians, Poles, and Germans. These became the urban white elephants where the diehard priests, such as Joe, chose to minister to the urban poor and the dwindling Sunday suburbanites who kept faith with their city parishes. The first of the new venues of secular American worship, an enclosed shopping mall, opened in 1956, reflecting and contributing to lifestyles and demographics that left dark centers in urban areas where Joe would choose to work. While the signs of the changing conditions that would collide with Joe's adulthood were ubiquitous, they were also invisible in their portents. At the foot of Main Street, a lake steamship, the *Canadiana*, used to ply an eleven mile stretch of Lake Erie each summer day between Buffalo and Crystal Beach, a large amusement park on the Canadian shore. It was a minor adventure to take the number eight bus to the end of the line, then board the boat for a day at the park. In 1956, it all ended when a racially charged brawl halted the trips. Nearly fifty years passed before the efforts to restore the grand old ship were finally abandoned. We all knew the fight was a problem but few understood it as an omen.

Joe enrolled in Canisius College in 1950 and graduated four years later. He was the first in our family to set foot on a college campus. I have no recollection of any discussion of a school other than Canisius, nor do I recall ever distinguishing between college and Canisius. Perhaps college alone was such a major step in our world that the distinction wasn't really made by any of us. It is also quite likely that the question was never considered seriously. College tuition was not within our family's means to begin with, and leaving town or attending UB (which was then private, secular, and expensive) were not real options. The cost issue resulted in what are some of my more vivid memories of Joe during those years; to get through, he worked part-time every spare hour during the school year and long and hard in the summers. My father helped, but Joe took on the lion's share of the burden.

The jobs I remember include his driving a delivery truck for Dates Laundry, carrying mail during the Christmas season rush, and summer work at Buffalo Carpenter Container, a rough and dirty job in a very low rent area somewhere near Ohio Street.

Dinnertime conversations often included what to me were fascinating tales of people and adventures from those places. On the light side were tales from the laundry route. I still carry the image from the story he told of the lady on his route with poor hearing. She would watch television during the day and couldn't hear the doorbell. In order not to startle her he would enter the house and shoot rubber bands at her until he got her attention. But far and away, most intriguing for me and, I think, for Joe, was the barrel factory (Buffalo Carpenter Container). In the early days of the first summer he would show his hands at dinner while we gawked in amazement at purple and swollen bruises and blisters. One of his jobs was forcing steel hoops and rims onto the newly formed barrels. The technology for this process was jamming them on with the heels of the hand. Until his hands toughened up, he was a mess. This was long before OSHA. Jim Cullen, who lived across the street, worked with Joe, at least during the first summer. Several times I remember riding down in the afternoon with my father to pick up Joe and returning instead with Jim. Joe would have had an opportunity to work overtime and, as always, took it.

His co-workers and their lives were endlessly fascinating to Joe. He would tell of the physical strength and toughness of men who did this work all their lives and marvel at their habits — ranging from loading hot pepper on their spaghetti to getting drunk on payday and staying that way until Monday morning. And they, in return, showed amusement and respect for "Big Red," the college kid who, when his blisters calloused over, would match them barrel for barrel and then work overtime. He may have been learning then about the hardship and bleakness of life for countless families who rarely come to public attention when we rhapsodize about free enterprise and the American dream.

Joe (center) and classmate Eugene Conley, prepare for their "Defense of Epistemology" with instructor Mr. John Giles Milhaven.

I was then busy mismanaging my adolescence, while Joe was at Canisius College beginning another academic career that would impress faculty and fellow students, to say nothing of his family. He seemed to come into his own in college where his integrity, combined with valued leadership qualities, earned him solid respect and admiration among his classmates. In 1954, Joe's senior year, the *Azuwur* college year book recorded powerful testimony to the esteem in which he was held by classmates and faculty. The section on the senior class opens with a full-page picture of Joe, the recipient that year of an award called "Ideal Man." It was described as follows:

> This most extraordinary award ... is given to the Senior, if there be any, who in the opinion of the faculty and members of the Senior class is outstanding in character and achievements in and out of class during his course at Canisius. This year the recipient of this great honor was A. Joseph Bissonette, president of the Senior class. Because of his scholastic and extra-curricular accomplishments he was thought worthy to be exalted above all his fellows.

One might have foreseen his capture of this award when, in his junior year, he was tapped for the College Honor Society, *Di Gamma*, a recognition of outstanding leadership and scholarship normally conferred on seniors or alumni who distinguished themselves after graduation.

As one would expect, Joe was active as a participant and leader in many extra-curricular activities, but some, for me, were clear fore-shadowings of the man others and I came to know as an adult. The sodality, in which he participated throughout college, is virtually unknown today. But its mission was to provide young men with the will and tools to carry the principles of their faith into action in their full round of associations and relationships. Another probably extinct group was the Aquinas Club, whose members studied the concept of freedom in the writings of Aquinas, Kant, Locke, Plato, Aristotle, and Descartes. From Joe's behavior in later years it is easy enough to see in these activities both a formative role and strong appeal to a young man seeking the spiritual and intellectual foundation for a life in the service of freedom and justice. Of course, then he couldn't know that more fame would accrue to those who articulated those principles rather than lived them.

But that's only part of the picture. One looks further and finds involvement with perhaps equal passion in the Glee Club and intramural sports. Joe's intramural basketball team, "the Butchers," went undefeated in their senior year, winning the championship. The Glee Club then, as during my years, was demanding in time but its modest rigors were more than offset by camaraderie, satisfaction, and plenty of socializing. Glee Clubbers were new-world student princes and the poor man's Whiffenpoofs. Those dimensions of his extra-curricular time were also reflective of personal characteristics unknown to many who remember mostly a man given to self-sacrifice and untiring, albeit often winless, advocacy for others — a tempting profile of a plaster saint. But Joe

IDEAL MAN

The college handbook describes the Ideal Canisius Man Award this way: *"This most extraordinary award, presented at the annual Junior Prom, is given to the Senior, if there be any, who in the opinion of the faculty and members of the Senior class is outstanding in character and achievements in and out of class during his course at Canisius."*

This year the recipient of this great honor was A. Joseph Bissonette, president of the Senior class. Because of his scholastic and extra-curricular accomplishments he was thought worthy to be exalted above all his fellows.

Above: Canisius College's Ideal Man,1954.
Inset, right: With Roberta Striegel at the Senior Prom.

was fun. I have said often, but it bears repeating, no one loved a cold beer and warm fire more than he did. Where he differed from most of us was in his inability to enjoy them fully while others were cold and thirsty. There he had a problem, as did many close to him who could never understand why he couldn't arrive earlier and stay later. After all, once the ceremonial duties were done, why couldn't he just relax and settle in? Only after his death did it become clear to me why he couldn't just "settle in." He was quietly but busily carrying out his vocation as he construed it. The sick, the lonely, the bereaved — all had first claim on Joe's time and energy. For many months after his death I met the people who knew where Joe was going when he refused the second beer. He was meeting with the people who were fighting "red lining" by fire insurance underwriters, attempting to dissuade grocery chains from closing inner city stores, negotiating a delay in the relocation of Trico, a multinational corporation that was among the first to join the parade to sources of cheap labor by relocating to the Mexican border.

But the most poignant expressions of grief and gratitude came from the families and individuals for whom his presence during times of trouble was as reassuring and comforting as it was predictable. Still, the fun part of his personality not only remained through most of his years in the priesthood but even grew. Rarely does one hear it, but some biblical scholars see Jesus portrayed in the Gospels as light-hearted and humorous. I have no idea of the accuracy of that history, but, to the extent of its validity, Joe's effort to imitate Jesus was even closer to the mark.

CHAPTER SEVEN

THE VOCATION AND THE LADIES

During our years growing up, we were given to believe that a vocation to the priesthood was some dramatic event that overwhelmed you like a spell. After Joe recognized his vocation, he knew and made it quite clear to anyone who cared to know that no magic force was involved, just a lengthy, difficult, deliberate decision. I know that, in his view, anything other than that was more in the realm of fantasy than reasoned choice, and probably not to be trusted.

This perspective on the vocation would foreshadow his experience and behavior as a priest — a lot of hard decisions with no skids greased by supernatural interventions and plenty of opposition from very natural interference. Much of this is clear from this partial characterization by his parishioners in the program for his twenty-fifth ordination anniversary celebrated at St. Bartholomew's April, 24, 1983.

> The vocation was a long and painful process ending in a decision in which self-interest was passed over for a higher purpose. Since that time, decisions and actions of that kind have become his hallmark. Convenient compromises could have brought material comforts, favor among the 'right' people, and other rewards along the path of least resistance. Instead of that path he chose a less traveled road, guided by principle and conviction. It is, therefore, no coincidence that, like another long ago whom he chose to follow, he shares bread with fishermen but might have dined with princes. Indeed, he seems to have failed completely to move among the aristocracy. But perhaps there is another aristocracy. Let us view Father Bissonette's "failure" in the context of words written long ago by a great English writer, E.M. Forster: 'I believe in aristocracy … though not an aristocracy of power based on rank and influence but an aristocracy of the sensitive, the considerate, and the plucky. Its members … represent the true human tradition, the one permanent victory of our queer race over cruelty and chaos. Thousands of them perish in obscurity, a few are great names. They are sensitive for each other as well as for themselves, they are considerate without being fussy, their power is to endure, and they can take a joke.'
>
> Mr. Forster and Father Bissonette never met but

> the image of the vine and branches captures the philosophy of both. Each spoke of commitment and the courage to take the consequences. Because one of them chose to live that philosophy, we are the aristocracy.

For Joe, this decision was taking shape amid all the typical involvements and interests of a healthy, attractive collegian. His high school ambition "to have a date" was realized in his college years. There were several girls in his life in that period. One, a friend of Joanne's, was quite taken with Joe, judging from the single Forget-Me-Not she had delivered daily while she was in Florida for several months. Another, Pat Noteman, seemed very much the object of his affections for a year or more. That relationship included a drive to Detroit for a reunion after she relocated. But the most enduring and serious that I recall was with Roberta Striegel, whom he dated right through the end of his senior year and up to the point where his decision to enter the seminary was firm. Indeed, it even accidentally extended briefly into his first year in the seminary. During his first Christmas at home from Christ the King Seminary, he attended a party whose guests included "Bobbie." Apparently thinking it amusing, some of their mutual friends arranged the departure plans so that he had to drive her home. He later characterized that situation as one of the toughest of his life. His vocation was put to the test and he told me at the time, it was a wrenching and close decision as to whether to return or come home. He did not share in the amusement of his friends who set it up. The young man whose adolescent social ambition was to have a date had come into his own as a young adult. The true extent of this appeared quite by accident in a note from the wife of one of Joe's college classmates. In January 2001, Mary Brown, who was one of Joe's contemporaries, wrote a brief, unsolicited recollection of the still shy but increasingly popular collegian: "Joe was very special. I remember when he and Bobbie were an item — stars in their own light! At CYO [Catholic Youth Organization] dances, all eyes were on them, including mine."

Among the women whom I recall was one who indirectly caused the destruction of the front end of Dad's 1953 Studebaker, our father's first and only new car. Perhaps providentially, the incident followed his death by several months. Joe was dating a young woman who lived in Niagara Falls whose father was rumored to be involved in organized crime. While at their home to pick her up for a date, the father backed out of the garage hurriedly and collided with the Studebaker that Joe had parked in the driveway. According to Joe, he was quite gracious about it and covered the repair bill with a check; there was no insurance company involved. I don't remember how or why that relationship ended but I do remember Joe's marveling at the fact that she didn't drink at all due to a pledge she had made at her father's behest to abstain until the age of twenty-five in return for some fairly attractive reward.

The dating was short lived but the charm and attractiveness to the ladies was to continue throughout his life, at times creating problems for them and him. While it was not at all comparable as a test of his vocation, there were other competing attractions, one of which I particularly remember. Toward the end of his senior year he was asked to speak at an event that I believe was a communion breakfast. Following the breakfast, a man approached him with an interesting proposal. He owned an automobile dealership and invited Joe to join his staff in the expectation that he would work his way into an ownership position in time. As Joe explained it, the man had no children and was literally seeking an heir to his business. I remember that so vividly because I couldn't fathom Joe's lack of interest without at least exploring it further. At the time Joe's vocation was a near certainty but neither I nor anyone else knew it.

In July of 1953, I had just finished grammar school at P.S. 63, and Joe was about to enter his last year at Canisius College. On the evening of July18, I had been hanging out in the neighborhood and returned home to find the house immaculate and my father sitting in the living room drinking a beer, a rare behavior for him, but it was a hot summer night and he had just finished scrubbing the kitchen floor; the last step in a complete housecleaning. The clean up that night was in anticipation of my mother's return from Lockport where she had spent the weekend with her parents. Dad could not easily verbalize his joy at her imminent return but the special effort around the house said it clearly enough. Minutes later he was in the bathroom sick to his stomach. I worried and he was angry. Rarely if ever had I or any of us seen him sick, and he liked it that way. He and I both went to bed but neither slept. From my room I could hear him tossing in his bed and eventually went down to the kitchen to prepare one of our family panaceas — a bowl of ice water and a wash cloth, which I delivered to his room then made my escape as quickly as possible. His being sick terrified me and I was alone. Joe was out somewhere and Joanne was at Sunset Bay with her sorority from high school. A few minutes later he called to me to phone the doctor. Not only was Dad never sick but he assiduously avoided doctors. My reaction was panic. I went to the first floor to call but could barely read the phone book. Then he called again and reminded me that there was a phone on the second floor in Joanne's room near him. I knew that but didn't want to be there and wished desperately for Joe to come home. Soon I heard the voices from across the street. It was Joe and Jim Cullen standing on the sidewalk talking, as was their habit. Joe came in and we finally succeeded in locating the doctor. Vividly I remember my enormous relief followed by more fear when I asked Dr. Lyons if it was "serious." Expecting to be reassured, I was instead told it was very serious. It was time for the priest. We had no luck rousing anyone at St. Joseph's (it was now after eleven P.M.) so I rode up on my bike and rang the bell at the rectory until I woke the priest who followed me home and administered last rites in the bedroom. Meanwhile, the ambulance had arrived, and as Dad was being carried out the front door he kept repeating, "Take care of Raymond." He must have known he wasn't coming back, and I think I did too.

Dad died in the hospital and I don't recall how we found out, but soon Joe and I were on our way in the Studebaker to Lockport. On the way down Joe told me I could cry if I felt like it but I couldn't. When we reached my grandparents' house I wouldn't go in at first; that was the big brother's job. Most of what I recall was my mother's entreaties to go to the hospital and Joe's insisting gently that it was too late. Throughout this, my grandfather pursued a fly through the living room with a swatter. Later, Joe and I drove to the home of Ed Sharkey, our mother's brother. It was the middle of the night, so we went to the backyard and threw pebbles against the second floor window until he finally awoke and said, "What the hell is going on?" We were all about to learn.

Dad's death changed everything but was to have an immediate impact on the course of Joe's life. He had been planning to enter the Jesuits but decided to become a diocesan priest to ensure his ability to remain in the area to help out. From then until he died, outside of his seminary days, it was a rare week that he didn't find time to spend an afternoon or evening with "Ma."

The change in direction was more than we knew. He presented it as a minor adjustment to accommodate the new circumstances, while in fact he had hoped to combine his priesthood with his love of learning and work in education. For a few years, he got his wish, but his own failure to "learn" would remove him from the classroom and nearly from the priesthood as well.

Above, left to right: Jim Cullen, Jim O'Leary, Tom O'Leary, and Joe en route to Virginia, 1953.

CHAPTER EIGHT

THE SEMINARY

In the fall of 1954, Joe entered Christ the King Seminary in Olean, N.Y., a town about 70 miles south of Buffalo. At the same time I was attending Canisius High School, where I was never planning to go, but my father's death changed my direction as well. Overwhelmed by her widowhood, my mother sought security for us wherever it could be found. For me, it was the known entity of the high school where Joe had been. It was a place where discipline would, my mother believed, lighten at least one burden as she struggled to manage her terrifying new responsibilities. Joanne was by then finished at Sacred Heart Academy and taking courses part-time at Canisius College while working as a secretary at Westinghouse.

My most salient memory of Joe during that first seminary year was his appearance when he arrived home for Christmas vacation. I awaited his return with great anticipation. No one in our family had ever been away for an extended time. Certainly my excitement was fueled mostly by eagerness to tell him all the entertaining events of my time at his old *alma mater.* In my perfect self-absorption I didn't notice any overt boredom with my endless tales, but he probably kept that under wraps then as he always did. The physical change of which we had heard but not yet seen, was striking. He had gained twenty-five pounds from September to December. On his six foot three inch frame it was easily accommodated: in fact, he looked quite massive.

My recollection of him during those years is limited, probably by my preoccupation with my own life as I completed high school and began Canisius College. I do not remember seriously considering an alternative school, nor do I recall being sold on college at all. One Saturday morning during senior year in high school, my friend, Tom Burke, and I took the alumni scholarship examination. I went because Tom was driving. Otherwise I would never have bothered. Joe had taken special classes in high school to prepare for scholarship support and didn't get any. I attended one class then dropped out. A month or so after the exam, I was summoned home by a very excited mother who announced that I had won a half tuition scholarship. The next day it became full, and I went to Canisius College just like my big brother, but on the cheap.

Remarkably, despite Joe's outstanding record at Canisius, there was little if any of the "Why can't you be like your brother?" attitude, at least that I recognized. But clearly there were those among the faculty who remembered him fondly and certainly noticed the difference. I believe it was during my first year in college and Joe's third year in the seminary that the first sign of his problem with the arbitrary exercise of authority appeared. He was home for a break, perhaps at Easter time, when my mother received a call with a message that he was to return to the seminary to participate in some ceremony for a visiting dignitary. Joe was incensed that he and others would have their vacations invaded for such frivolous pomp. He apparently pretended not to have received the message and the day of the event he went to the zoo. While there, he, of course, ran into one of the senior administrators of the seminary. He was disciplined severely, but never let on that it was significant. Customarily, third year seminarians receive their so-called minor orders by which the status of Deacon is conferred. Joe was excluded from that for his willful insubordination but described it as a minor formality that would be remedied the next year at ordination anyway. Only later did I learn that it was a major punishment, but I never knew if he considered it so and played it down for our sake, or if he in fact saw it as trifling.

During Joe's first year in the seminary, many miles away in Montgomery, Alabama, a relatively minor incident took place that was to effect a sea change in domestic and even world society.

Whether Joe had more than a passing awareness of the event or even began to appreciate its significance can only be surmised.

A 42 year-old black seamstress named Rosa Parks refused a bus driver's order to move to the rear of the Cleveland Street bus as she headed home from work. Others had done it, but they didn't have the characteristics sought by the local NAACP which, at the time, was looking for an opportunity to make a test case of the discrimination in public transportation. Rosa was a gift — a respectable, courageous, and politically aware black citizen who would underscore the injustice of the system. Coupled with Rosa Park's sudden availability was the presence in town of a new minister at the Dexter Avenue Baptist Church, Martin Luther King, Jr. The afternoon of Parks's expected conviction, the Montgomery Improvement Association was formed to follow up on the case. To avoid slighting any existing black leaders, the chairmanship was given to the Reverend Mr. King. The result was the dismantling of formalized racist policies in the South and the emergence of a leader who articulated the central concept informing Joe's beliefs and career as an advocate for civil rights: while you help the victims of unjust policies, search out and destroy the systemic policies — the structures — that create and perpetuate them. King was to die violently at the hands of his enemies; the young men who killed Joe murdered one of their best friends.

CHAPTER NINE

A PRIEST IN THE FAMILY

Joe was ordained in the spring of 1958. The formalities were pat. On Saturday of the weekend, the newly graduated seminarians would receive Holy Orders; a rite conducted by their Bishop. I recall only fragments of that event, but one part of the rite annoyed me then and strikes me now in its irony. Toward the culmination of the rite, the seminarians prostrated themselves before the Bishop and, at a signal from one of the officiating priests, would rise in unison. Well they didn't rise in unison. Anxious and over-eager, their heads began to pop up randomly as they looked about to avoid missing the cue. To me, the confusion marred what promised to be a great dramatic finish. Little did I guess that the imperfect demonstration of obedience and submission would be played out in real life years later, as young priests living through the iconoclasm of the 1960s left the priesthood in unprecedented numbers in the decade to follow. Equally ignorant was I that Joe's later disobedience may have had symbolic roots in those early missed cues.

Joe chose to remain a priest but not on the terms of abject obeisance to hierarchical authority. Throughout his career, his head would come up at the wrong time as he searched the streets and his own conscience for signals as to when and how to meet his definition of a follower of Christ. That definition also became apparent that weekend. Following ordination, families typically hosted a breakfast-reception during which the newly ordained priest would speak to friends and relatives. Joe used a metaphor from Scripture likening the Church, Christ's body, to a grapevine. Well I remember the intensity of his words as he repeated Christ's admonition, "I am the vine and you are the branches; without me you are nothing." He leaned hard on the word "nothing," an emphasis that would endure. Throughout his life he remained faithful to that belief despite countless temptations, indeed invitations, from outside and within the Church to disconnect. What would be the culminating evolution of this position appeared in a sermon delivered 26 years later during Peace Week in 1984: "God has called us to build the kingdom of justice and peace on earth. We are responsible — and it is an awesome responsibility. God will guide us and strengthen us for the task, but He will not do it for us." Those statements taken together are clear signals that Joe never saw his or our connection to Christ as some passive admiration.

After the breakfast, Joe went home to our house on West Northrup and spent much of the afternoon chopping ice from the front walk. He was working off his anxiety about his first Mass the following morning. The next morning his hands were raw with blisters, a lot like the old days at Buffalo Carpenter Container.

Following the first Mass at St. Joseph's on Sunday, there was a large reception in the school hall. It was crowded with friends, relatives, and members of the parish. I recall a sense of something huge and significant having occurred and felt washed in reflected pride. A ritual at the reception was the blessing by the new priests. The line was long but I waited gladly to receive this special gift from my big brother and then stood in another line for the blessing from Joe's classmate and best friend, Jack Weimer. Two blessings in one day by men I admired and knew conferred a huge sense of pride and doubtless contributed to an inflated sense of significance that was not easily contained, or contained at all. Instead, it was dramatized for my own friends as though my trifling responsibilities were key to the success of the occasion. Since I really had little to do, I scurried about chain smoking and sighing dramatically to convey the great pressure on me. I must have wanted badly to have a real part in it all.

It was the custom then to place new priests in a program called the missionary apostolate. Essentially, they were rotated through outlying Western New York communities where permanent assignment of priests was not feasible but a presence was needed. Of course, it was also "boot camp" for the novices. Joe's first assignment was at St. Mark's in Rushford, N.Y., a small town about an hour's drive south of Buffalo. Rushford was a resort community on a small lake. The population swelled in the summer, and the need for a priest expanded accordingly. It was a brief stay and he was back in Buffalo by September of 1958 for assignment to a local parish, St. Joseph's in North Tonawanda, in the role of assistant pastor and trainee.

As we were learning through his stories about parish life, we were also learning things about Joe whose significance would remain opaque for years, to him as well as those of us who "followed" his career. Joe had and maintained an almost naïve trust in people long after he might have lost it through experience. It was almost his trademark and probably the cause of his death. A telling sign came early and potently.

Joe's "pastoral counseling" experience began in earnest with a young woman at St. Joseph's. During his visits home she was the subject of several references to his new life as an assistant pastor. The story was of a disillusioned young wife and mother whose husband was not communicative, a condition probably similar to failing to "understand" her. Joe would not then nor ever be caught ignoring the call of someone requiring so little as a bit of his time and a lot of his understanding. One evening she was at our house on Northrup where we made ourselves scarce so the conversation could go on with minimal interruption. But it was a small house so her presence and the intensity of the discussion were not easily concealed, even from me. She stayed a long time and the seriousness of her communication problems at home was evident. Not long thereafter, the counseling sessions ceased and we learned that her communication problems at home were indistinguishable from her infatuation with Joe.

What effect this experience had on Joe's future relationships with women, I don't know, but I do recall several references to certain women who, in today's idiom, "came on" to priests because they were seen as safe and maybe even a risk-free challenge to their sex appeal. I'm certain the woman from St. Joseph's was not in this category, but he was clearly learning how many complications of celibacy were not listed in the textbooks.

Joe took seriously Christ's invitation to shed worldly goods and follow. Combined with a natural generosity, it explained a lot of what people remember about him. You always had a balance of payments problem with Joe despite the fact that he appeared to have little of material value to give. Some time during that year, a life-long pattern became very evident. Following ordination, it was customary for all the new priests to buy a new car through some quantity purchase arrangement with the diocese. Joe got his first of the two new cars of his life, and the second new car ever to live in our family garage. It was a 1958 Chevrolet Biscayne, priestly black, with one optional piece of equipment, a radio. Shortly before his death in 1953, my father had purchased the first new car of his life, a 1953 Studebaker Commander. My mother had been driving that car as she struggled to patch together an income from the leftovers of my father's insurance business. Never a trouble-free car in the first place, it was becoming increasingly problematic and a cause of concern as she often traveled to unfamiliar places in the evening to call on clients. Soon she was driving a 1958 Chevrolet and Joe had the Studebaker, in time for the full flowering of planned obsolescence to emerge. With the exception of one other period of a new, stripped-down 1971 Chevrolet, the pattern was always the same — when Joe got a new car it went to my mother and he took over the remains of what had been his new car several years earlier.

Aside from its reflection of his very genuine generosity, it represented a consistent pattern of self-sacrifice that never changed. By driving a five-year-old car in those days, in Buffalo weather, you were guaranteed only one non-stop feature — headaches. In fact, car stories, always bad, were one of the most routine subjects of conversation when we were together as adults. That year, in particular, was difficult for Joe. He began his second tour of the missionary apostolate in East Otto, N.Y., a community an hour and a half by car in those days, if the car completed the trip. Also around that time began a pattern of Sunday afternoon visits to Mom. Driving an unreliable car between East Otto and Buffalo every Sunday became an unpleasant ordeal throughout much of the winter and when he did finally return late on Sunday nights, he would spend the night and the rest of the week in an unheated apartment over a vacant store. He slept many nights in his clothes and that Christmas his major gift was an electric blanket. Ordinarily this would have been an unacceptable luxury but he took and used it without protest.

Just after Joe's death, Monsignor John Zeitler, a friend of Joe's from childhood and fellow priest, told me of an old folk tale that Joe would liken to his relationship with me. Of course, I had never known of this from Joe. The story was too old for O. Henry authorship, but had that kind of twist. In it, two brothers worked poor adjoining farms. Surreptitiously, the older brother would frequently go out at night and add grain to his brother's bin. One night, he was discovered by his younger brother, who was also outside because he had been secretly doing the same thing for him. I was astonished to hear of this, but was instantly reminded of one of Joe's little tricks so typical of his lifelong pattern of generosity, real generosity — the kind done in secret to preclude indebtedness or even gratitude. While I was in graduate school, I spent some of my summers at our mother's apartment at Marine Drive. Joe and I had a habit of placing our wallets on the buffet top when we were there. Normally, before leaving at night to stimulate the economy of local watering holes, I'd check my wallet to see how late I'd be out. Often I'd discover a few more dollars than I had expected. Eventually the mystery was solved when I caught Joe slipping the bills into my wallet and, when questioned, pretending to have gotten the wallets mixed up. I can't remember any reciprocal behavior on my part to parallel the behavior of the farmers in the story, but Joe apparently saw or imagined it. The generosity was not limited to me but was part of his personality for as long as I recall. Throughout this story is a theme reflecting a choice to follow Christ. Of course, we know that such a decision for most would be symbolic or metaphorical, but Joe appears to have taken it literally. The wallet, the tax return, the loans and sales that were really gifts all fit that picture. The anecdotes scattered throughout are bolstered by the closest thing I have to documentary evidence. Joe's last checkbook covering the ten months preceding his death is quite remarkable. In that ten-month period I can find not a single purchase of anything resembling personal acquisition. Nearly every expenditure is for contributions, education (workshops and seminars and retreats), birthday gifts for his family, car repairs, and low balance fees to the bank. The only thing approaching a personal purchase is what appears to be a monthly outlay for liquor. Joe drank only socially as did his friends, but being caught without a bottle of decent Scotch when Bill Stanton visited would have placed him at serious risk of verbal abuse. (Monsignor Stanton was a close friend of Joe's who died in early 2004.) Keeping a supply of liquor on hand for guests was typical, and he never arrived anywhere for a meal without a bagful of "contributions." But, the story in the checks is not complete without noting the several loans to a close friend, one of which was $400 (about $800 in today's dollars) when his balance was $1185. His view of the purpose of money is sharp and consistent.

But his definition was also highly exclusionary. While he spent little on himself, probably considering it indulgent, he abhorred waste and could not abide losing a penny to institutional greed or ineptitude. His campaign against a parking ticket received while visiting my mother at Marine Drive is just one example. His unjust ticket took him to the Parking Violations Bureau armed with photographic "evidence" of the unwarranted citation. He won his case but at a cost in time and effort probably exceeding the fine. He knew that and was angry about it, but would not let it pass, and rarely did. Monsignor Bill Stanton never missed an opportunity to tell about convincing Joe to accompany Jack Weimer, Pat Keleher, fellow priests and traveling companions, and himself on a trip to California. There were hard negotiations in advance about the level of accommodations. Bill prevailed, as he tells it, on indoor plumbing, but about little else. While settling into a seedy hotel in Los Angeles, Joe opened the blinds and pointed triumphantly, announcing to his grumbling companions how well they were situated in that they could see the Hilton from their window.

His foolishness about money was far larger than altruism or depression era thrift. His message at ordination about following Christ required, for him, not only divestiture of material things and their attendant distractions, but releasing himself from the constraints of being number one. In their workbook, *A Pilgrim's Progress*, Timothy Alan and Elizabeth Goodine offer an insightful interpretation of how this worked in Joe.

> ... he had embraced a vision of life and church which led him along a path to an increasingly deeper awareness of and sensitivity to the needs of others. As this awareness of others, of community, grew, so did a parallel development — renunciation of things of the world, denial and

> emptying of self — especially with regard to his own needs. Always more for others, always less for himself — Joe invested the essential stuff of his own life in these complementary visions of his place as a priest and human being. This complementarity never did work out to an equilibrium that would satisfy and comfort those who loved and cared about him. For Joe, however, this was the way it had to be. He was too deeply committed to his journey along the path toward the Kingdom of God on earth. He was too concerned and worried about those who journeyed with him to allow his attention to waiver from them and the destination to himself. Finally, less and more converged in an emptying out of his own life. Everything possible having been renounced, less became absolute even as he was in the act of giving more bread to the hungry. Ultimate less-ness, ultimate more-ness — Joe Bissonette's life ended at the precise point where these commitments intersected.

But the consequences of his altruism were not always benign. The costs were also larger than money. Accepting advocacy for the marginal invariably meant antagonizing the influential both in the community and his own Church. That cost him whatever dreams he had of conducting his ministry with the blessing and support of the Church leadership. It also cost him his life when he opened his door to one too many persons seeking his help. The "foolishness" of opening the door the night of February 24,1987 was not an isolated incident, either in general or with regard to his killers. Teddy Simmons chose that door because he had reason to believe it would open.

CHAPTER TEN

ALWAYS READING DEM BOOKS

Another of his early assignments as an assistant pastor was at Queen of Martyrs, a predominantly Polish parish in Cheektowaga, a suburb of Buffalo. The pastor apparently found Joe's habit of reading for recreation as well as personal development unusual and, perhaps, amusing. Joe certainly found the pastor's reaction amusing and used to imitate his heavily accented comments, "Fadder Bissonette, you are always reading dem books." For Joe and the family it was a good laugh. But for me at the time it was also a rude awakening. Until then I had always thought of priests as somewhat bookish if not at least intellectually inclined. The consequences of Joe's decision not to enter the Jesuit order were becoming increasingly apparent. Frequently, I wondered if his proclivity to seek and inquire was unhealthy for him in a hierarchical environment where learning was not a central value. It was the kind of behavior and attitude ill suited to a system steeped in authority, status, and obedience. It may have been equally troublesome in a religious community, but, as a Jesuit, he may have found intellectual curiosity less threatening to those in authority, if not to some of his peers as well.

Learning notwithstanding, Joe was certainly beginning his acquaintance with the peculiarities and pathologies visited on many aging celibate men reigning over religious and secular fiefdoms. The peculiarities emerged almost immediately. At Queen of Martyrs the housekeeper was a frequent subject of Joe's ire, as he was subjected to an endless parade of ruined meals. She was given to bring every meal and those partaking of it to their knees by overcooking. I can still hear Joe's exasperated comment, "She cooks the hell out of everything and Kulpinski (the pastor) excuses it because (in Polish accent) 'She is not a very good cook but a morally good woman.' " How he would endlessly suffer the bad cooking because of the moral character of the perpetrator was incomprehensible to Joe; he could not comprehend the presumed mutual exclusivity of morality and culinary competence. His frustration was more than irritation with the food; it was also part of a certain rigidity of both youth and his new role in life. I once read an analysis of the developmental stages of physicians that I think probably applies to most professions and certainly fit Joe's pattern. The analysis describes three stages: the romance period characterized by a strong emotional embrace of the new status and the tenets of the profession; the precision phase in which one adheres strictly to the received scientific basis of the profession; and the period of synthesis in which experience and wisdom become the principal guides to one's attitude and practice. Joe was solidly in the romance and precision phases of his priesthood as I recall his early years following ordination. The enthusiasm of the romance phase took the form of a fairly rigid view of Catholic dogma. Small incidents come to mind which, at the time, seemed perfectly normal and natural to be known and practiced by our resident expert on the way things were in God's eyes.

My aunt Lorrine was my father's sister. Some time before I was born, she left her husband and, with her two young children, returned to the family homestead at 314 Wyoming Avenue in Buffalo. She raised her children to adulthood and met a widower named Ed Lang. Ed had become quite well off financially through his candy business (Lang's Orange Chocolate) and, later, selling mutual funds. Lorrine's husband had not been heard from for years, but neither was he known to be dead. By Church law, therefore, she could not remarry. They did anyway but with full knowledge that it was outside the Church and could not be condoned by the family. Joe was quite matter-of-fact about the situation, stating simply that we could not be a party to the non-wedding. Whether he shared the family's sympathy for Lorrine's plight I don't recall, but the general feeling was that she was fully justified in her choice after spending most of her adult life as a de facto widow. No one begrudged her a partner, nor did they overtly question the rules; it was just thought to be an unfortunate but irreparable situation. Interestingly, Joe, the family authority on such things, held to the straight application of the law and did not, to my recollection, question its wisdom. This was a much younger version of the priest whose career hallmark was challenging arbitrary authority, ecclesiastical and secular. The family acceptance of the marriage occurred gradually and incrementally as Ed and Lorrine entertained family, including ours, in their new home. I remember wondering, when we were first invited to dinner, if Joe would object. He didn't and the tacit "blessing" of the illicit union was complete.

In my life, I have never visited a gravesite, including Joe's. I think I learned that from him shortly after our father died when somehow the subject came up and he stated quite unceremoniously, "There's no one there." To me that made perfectly good sense, but it may have been a cold reality for my mother. Of course it was the Church's position that, in this case, coincided in its effect with the belief of those professing no religion at all. At the time he was still a seminarian but the doctrinal "purity" persisted for several years.

This unquestioning adherence was apparently inconsistent with his already evident problem with capricious authority. But I think the disconnect was superficial. Joe's choice of the zoo over a reception for a dignitary at the seminary was a rejection of self-serving bureaucratic behavior. At this stage of his life he probably saw that as different from many of the canonical rules that were just as man-made but older.

The evolution of his early dogmatism is illustrated in an amusing story by Evelyn Brady, who recalls her first post Vatican II face-to-face confession. She chose Joe because they were only distantly acquainted. After relating her sins, she found herself arguing with her confessor who insisted they were not sins at all but simply mistakes.

Concurrent with his assignment to Queen of Martyrs, he served for about six months as backup chaplain for several of the city hospitals. I know he found this difficult and unsettling work. He remarked on several occasions how many months after that he would experience dread every time the phone rang in the night. Perhaps, however, it helped him in his pastoral work later. He was always there when someone was sick. He took that aspect of his pastoral role very seriously, which probably explains why he made so many friends among his parishioners and could never seem to find much time for himself, although I'm not sure he really tried. Typical of this dedication was the message of the black woman from the Perry Projects who approached me and my wife, Ann, following Joe's death. She told an amazing story of how Joe had become almost a father to her children and was, in her mind, responsible for the positive influences affecting her family. In the course of meeting many people like that after he died, I learned how many of those relationships he developed with his parishioners over the years. The priesthood was his life, not a job.

During this same period, Joe enrolled in a graduate program at

Canisius College for a master's degree in history. His thesis topic was the handling by the local news media, then two daily papers, of Al Smith's candidacy for President. Smith was the first serious Catholic contender for that office and bucked a powerful anti-Catholic bias in American politics. (As I write this, the Republican primary contest between George W. Bush and John McCain is focusing on McCain's suggestion that Bush's visit to Bob Jones University was an affront to Catholics.) His fascination with the Al Smith story was natural enough for a committed young Catholic who was continuing his intellectual development. But the thesis offers a perspective on decisions he made throughout life with respect to authority. When Joe had completed his course work and was well into writing his thesis, a new chairman was appointed in the history department, a new chairman who didn't like Joe's topic. He had to abandon all his work and begin again on a totally new thesis. He was angry, frustrated, and incredulous. But once the emotions settled, he went back to work researching the history of social welfare services in Erie County and eventually completed his first master's degree.

He believed the chairman's decision an arbitrary exercise of authority with no academic basis. Among his responses was serious consideration of quitting the program. Yet on reflection, he realized that to follow his impulses would be to shoot himself in the foot. Quitting would harm only him and sacrifice larger and more important goals in order to achieve the short-term satisfaction of walking out the door. Situations similarly frustrating and unfair would dog his life in the priesthood, but he knew that to accomplish his chosen goals he must work around, if not with, those in charge. His life showed a consistent pattern of suffering personal wrongs to better confront institutionalized injustice. However, each of these incidents surely added to the intensity of his feelings about fair play and capricious use of authority.

Joe participating in a rally against U.S. policies in El Salvador, ca. 1984.

Father Bissonette chats with Turner High School students, Marty Hamann, Pat Clemens, and Jerry Wrzosek (1964).

CHAPTER ELEVEN

IMPRESSIONABLE YOUNG MINDS

Joe's next move was a sharp departure from life as a parish priest. In 1960 he became head of religious education at Bishop Turner High School, one of several diocesan secondary schools. Located in a demographically changing section of Buffalo's east side, this school was probably his first significant involvement with the inner city. The assignment occurred about the time I left Buffalo for the University of Maryland, so my knowledge of his experience there is based on the recall of others and his own reminiscences later.

Based on his extensive personal commitment to education, one might have expected this to be a rewarding and fulfilling assignment. It might have been, but it was also roughly concurrent with the tenure of Bishop James McNulty, for whom Joe was at least an annoyance, if not a threat. Nonetheless, he appeared reasonably satisfied with the work and clearly made a powerful impression on many for his concern, integrity, and expectations of them. Yet more than one student recalled his apparent distraction, a sense that he would or should be elsewhere. With the exception of his efforts to reach the kids who were on or beyond the fringe of personal or academic trouble, he seemed to be doing his job without his heart in it. Perhaps he felt the front lines for him were not the classroom, and he brooded over his removal from the "community" and serving a shepherd whom he could neither follow nor respect.

This was also the period when he worked closely with Monsignors Jack Weimer and Bill Stanton, who were to become lifelong friends as well as fellow members of the obstreperous group of Buffalo priests who saw the Church's mission as far more than the traditional conduct of ecclesiastical rites. For Joe, and his kindred spirits, dealing with the poor and disenfranchised was at least as important as managing the sacraments. Linked closely with this perspective was disaffection from the rigid hierarchical structure of the Church. These sentiments set Joe on a collision course with Bishop McNulty, and many others within and related to the Church, who found the somewhat medieval system comfortable and convenient.

While at Turner, Joe had long-term influence on many of his

students. Jack O'Connor of "...how did they get the drop on him?" fame was one, and another was Dennis Horrigan, who became a friend of mine some years later. Shortly after Joe's death, Dennis wrote a letter to the editor of *The Buffalo News.* In it he remembered Joe's integrity and the unflinching adherence to principle that he practiced and modeled for his students. Dennis remembered Joe among the faculty as the "rock," at first glance an unlikely description of a man known for gentleness and non-violence. Dennis's letter was published in the *News* on March 4,1987, eight days after Joe's death. His words tell us a lot about how Joe's behavior and example affected at least one of his students and, in a more cynical vein, explain why a wary Bishop would want Joe far removed from impressionable young minds. Dennis spoke then as he does now, briefly and to the point:

> Father Joe Bissonette was our high school social studies teacher. He was a giant of a man in body and soul who spoke to us of social justice, peace, and making a commitment at a time when we didn't fully understand its meaning.
>
> We often referred to Father Joe as the 'rock' because of his strength and determination. Our paths have crossed many times through the years and each time it was clear that Father Joe's commitment and involvement with mankind, peace, and justice had become more intense. He was, as his close friend, Father Stanton, stated, 'our best,' the kind of man one imagines a saint to be. Father Joe had a profound impact on all who knew him. He brought out the best in all of us.

Importantly, however, one needs to recall that Joe's students were adolescents for whom much of what he said and did was a mystery then and, for some, still is. "Joe Biz," his name among the students, was something of an anomaly in many respects. His former students remember a generation later several curious things about him that may not be so odd in an historical context. A teacher of adolescent boys who never raised his voice is almost unheard of. To this day they recall that behavior with some amazement. When his class became unruly, Joe would turn his back and continue his lecture in a barely audible voice. He would also make clear that what he was saying "would be on the test," the primary, if not exclusive, criterion of intellectual curiosity for most students. Routinely, quiet and order would return and Joe would turn and continue as though nothing had happened.

Somewhere he learned an alternative to raising his voice, and I have to wonder if perhaps it was from our mother, whose voice none of us ever heard above conversational tone. Coupled with the controlled voice level were an apparent incapacity to get angry and an evenhanded approach to all the students. He managed difficult situations and students without raising his voice, losing his temper, or according special treatment, good or bad, to anyone. He seemed to have a few creative ways to get the attention of his adolescent audience. Ethnic slurs traded among the Italian, Irish, and Polish students, many of whom were from working class second-generation immigrant families, were part of the fabric at Turner. Joe's approach, that they quote today, was to simply and quietly say: "Put away the flags." For those in "jug," an after school hour of kneeling with hands in the air, Joe sometimes excused early anyone who could answer trivia questions such as "What Buffalo street crosses Main without changing its name?" It made an impression. Forty years later they remember the answer.

Although having no "pets," he did seem, in the memory of some students, to have an unusual tolerance for and maybe even affection for some of the more difficult students. Former students remember vividly his special concern and support for the kids in or heading for serious trouble. In the context of a life of advocacy for those on the fringe, this may have been nothing more than an early manifestation of that proclivity. At the time he was in his early thirties and already showing clear signs that, whatever his views on "pets," he would not be one and those he favored were likely to be strays or orphans.

It would be a mistake to attribute Joe's effectiveness as a disciplinarian simply to his being soft spoken. Along with the quiet manner was something else that the students could see but found difficult to describe. Dennis Horrigan draws a picture of a big guy who would stand at the window in front of the class and look calmly at his charges with an expression that clearly conveyed who was in charge and who was not. This manner was part of what he and others were reflecting in their use of the term "rock."

As a teacher, Joe was remembered for a puzzling, sometimes startling unevenness. During an uninspired lecture on social studies, he would suddenly come upon a subject or issue relating to social justice and the matter-of-fact presentation gave way to an impassioned jeremiad with notes and textbook temporarily ignored. The students were, of course, nonplussed by these rants, finding themselves confronted by a man and a passion totally new to them. What impact this had can only be guessed, but those who recall it tell of having their routine ways of thinking or not thinking about certain social issues challenged and changed at least for a minute.

The beginnings of racial integration in the 1960s were rough and ugly everywhere and Turner was no exception. At the time, one of the two Afro-American students in the school was a starter on the basketball team and one of the first black player in the Catholic League. Each time he stepped on the court, a racial epithet sounded from the stands and a fight ensued between the Turner fans and their opponents. And that behavior was not limited to the students. Modeling prejudice for the young people, coaches and other adults would find ways to demonstrate their own distaste for the integration of the team and the league. Joe would have been saddened and outraged by that display of intolerance, especially among people and organizations that putatively attach a premium to fair play. The experience surely contributed to his lifelong dedication to racial tolerance and profound disdain for its proponents.

Henry Conforti was a lay faculty member who had been a classmate of mine in college. Henry was not given to gratuitous compliments about anyone, but about Joe, he would frequently exclaim in his New York City accent, "Your brother was the best."

Following Joe's death, that statement was closely echoed by many of his colleagues. The verbatim echo was from Monsignor Pat Keleher outside St. Bartholomew's after Joe's funeral. Weeping openly, Pat, a friend and occasional traveling companion of Joe, Stanton, and Weimer, said simply to the TV reporter, "He was the best." Dennis Horrigan's "rock" theme was also heard repeatedly. Monsignor Jerry Sullivan, then coordinator of the inner city parishes, said, "We've lost the most consistently principled priest on peace and justice issues in the Diocese of Buffalo," and Bill Stanton, then pastor at St. Ambrose in south Buffalo, called him "the most courageous priest I know on any issue." Jack Weimer said Joe was his "conscience" and the ultimate compliment came from Ron Walker, a deacon at a neighboring east side parish: "He was a priest's priest."

At Turner, Joe chaired the religion department and moderated the Christian Student Association. From the text of the 1964 year book, Joe's words offer insights into his evolving view of the meaning of being a Christian. He described us as " ... spiritual Semites ... who suffer persecution with the primitive Christians ... burn with the missionary zeal of Paul, Boniface, and Xavier [and] mourn with the victims of Nero's lions and Chou En Lai's tiger." His activist perspective on religious values is reflected in his work with the Christian Student Association in which he urged students to apply the gospels to ecumenism, integration, technology, and personal relationships. His insistence that the study of religion is a waste if those values never leave the classroom surely anticipated the future ministry of the priest who would infuriate some of the Church hierarchy by his social activism, finding his pulpit on the steps of city hall as readily as before the altar.

Indeed this failure to compartmentalize his religious values was to mark the end of his teaching career. One afternoon in the mid sixties, Monsignor Bill Stanton, one of Joe's faculty colleagues at Turner and a close friend, was visited in his office by the principal, Father Schwab, who informed him that Joe had to go. Schwab had been told by the superintendent, Monsignor Leo Hammerl, that Joe was to be reassigned for several recent actions that rendered him unsuited to continue in a teaching role. According to Schwab, Joe's offenses were: participating in a march in Chicago protesting our involvement in the Vietnam War; signing a petition in support of the Berrigan brothers; and, in recognition of the spirit of Vatican II, challenging the Holy Name Society at Queen of Martyrs to integrate their religious principles into their daily lives. Following some discussion of reconsideration, Schwab called the superintendent in Bill's presence, but the decision was irrevocable. It was the certain conviction of Stanton, Joe, and others close to the situation that Joe's removal was for his seditious ideas and behavior that certainly could not be given a forum among young minds in formation. They were convinced that the official reasons given for his reassignment — urgent need for another priest at Immaculate Conception Parish, were fabrications. Nonetheless, Joe was reassigned as assistant pastor at Immaculate Conception, where his stay would also be interrrupted by his commitment to social justice. Joe went to the Chancery office to protest the action and apparently met with Auxiliary

Bishop McLaughlin who denied that the particulars enumerated by Schwab were related to the reassignment. He was told that Immaculate Conception, a lower west side parish, was in need of a priest to minister to its large and growing population of young people and denied the issues that had been relayed by Schwab. According to Stanton, Schwab had neither the motive nor imagination to have concocted those details, leaving him [Stanton] convinced that the tripartite indictment had indeed come from the Bishop.

At a subsequent Priest Senate meeting, the Bishop, James McNulty, confirmed the official posture of the Diocese alleging that Joe was needed at the parish to help minister to the young people. In issuing the reaffirmation of the official reason, he apparently could not resist tipping the hand, revealing his real motive for the transfer — Joe's unsuitability for influencing the thinking of young people. He was compelled to announce that, after Joe's arrival at Immaculate Conception, a young white lady [*sic*] in the parish was attacked by five Negro boys following a social gathering under parish auspices. The incident, despite its occurrence after the kids had left the parish property, was attributed to inadequate supervision by Joe. By the Bishop's report, Joe had been unable to explain the incident when subsequently called before a board of two bishops. The Bishop also announced at this meeting that Joe had received more opportunities for furthering his education than any priest in the Diocese. This observation was made in the context of suggesting that Joe had defaulted on the Bishop's investment in his education. Presumably, those educational experiences would have prepared Joe to prevent the incident in the first place. Apparently, neither the Bishop nor his auxiliary saw any inconsistency or irony in reassigning Joe from one youth ministry to another because he was an unwholesome influence on young people.

This meeting was on June 11, 1969, at an assembly of the Priest Senate, an organization formed several years earlier in response to a Vatican II call for improved bilateral communication between priests and their bishops. Bishop McNulty was an invited guest at this meeting and used it to publicly upbraid several rebellious priests, including Joe, for subversive behavior and concluded by "deferring all activity of the Senate until further notice." The minutes of the meeting reflect a highly contentious encounter in which the Bishop found it necessary to identify those "elements" in the Diocese who were opposing the authority of the Pope and his Bishop. The "further notice" did not come during Bishop McNulty's lifetime, which ended in 1973.

The Bishop was also very aware of Joe's increasing visibility as an opponent of the Vietnam War. Joe had been seen in a protest in Chicago and was the prominent signatory of a quarter page ad in *The Buffalo News*, calling for a cessation of U.S. involvement. The ad was signed by fifty members of the Priests' Association of Buffalo, but Joe's name was at the head of the list and not because it was alphabetized. Interestingly, this subversive public statement, calling for an end to American participation in the war, was supported by citations from established Church hierarchy —

the National Council of Catholic Bishops and several papal documents. Clearly, neither this statement nor Joe's ideas were rejections of or revolts against the Church, but calls to proclaim what he and others believed to be the Church's true spirit. He was quickly becoming an outspoken and high profile member of the anti-war faction, a group initially identified with hippies, draft resisters, and generally fringe malcontents of the nation. That he did this as both an individual and a priest was a problem for the Bishop whose flock included many sheep whose fleece resembled mink. Any chance that Joe would be "successful" in the Church hierarchy was stopped dead in those years. He was embarrassing and challenging his own boss. The boy whose father worried that he would not succeed for lack of combativeness was failing because of it. But this was a man who copied and saved a quote from the then notorious "power to the people" guru, Sol Alinsky: "Do you want to help people or do you want to be a Bishop?" For Joe, and others like him, success and courage would require a different yardstick.

For Bill Stanton, the yardstick was pretty clear. Joe was not only the most courageous but also the most confrontational priest in the Diocese. The confrontational aspect was contextual. Joe was exceedingly tolerant of personal human failings and seldom reproached individuals. His anger was aroused when he perceived institutionalized injustice, greed, and insensitivity on the part of those vested with public or corporate responsibility. In fact, to know him socially, you would find Stanton's words difficult to accept. Somewhat like his mother, Joe was self-effacing to the point of being, at times, excessively deferential to others. While this trait was consistent with his humility and generosity, it was not a quality one would associate with confrontation. But Stanton knew well how quickly Joe would place himself at risk where he saw exploitation and neglect. Nor did he do this without significant personal pain. Confrontation was not his style, but it was his job. It was no slip of the tongue when he took some liberty with the liturgy to amend the petition "protect us from *all* anxiety" to "protect us from *needless* anxiety." To live a life of integrity could never be entirely comfortable, so why ask.

In 1970, I returned to Buffalo after a ten-year absence that included graduate school, a tour of duty in the Army, and a job in Springfield, Massachusetts. During this time I had married and our first child, Matthew, was born while we were at Fort Sam Houston in San Antonio, Texas. My wife, Ann, had met Joe earlier once or twice, and he had celebrated our wedding Mass at Trinity Church in Washington, D.C., in February of 1966. When I returned, Joe was the assistant pastor at Immaculate Conception. The church is at the corner of Elmwood Avenue and Virginia Street and includes in its parish what is known as Buffalo's Allentown. Allentown is our Greenwich Village: an artsy, somewhat Bohemian, and trendy community with a broad mix of social, economic, and ethnic populations. The housing stock during Joe's tenure there included several blocks of quaint Victorian homes much sought after by people seeking urban living with charm. The rehabilitation of many of these homes was a gentrification process similar to what occurs in most cities when the appeal of suburbia reaches its limits for various people and reasons. Included in the parish, however, was Buffalo's lower west side, an area then and now resembling, in many respects, a third world country. Poverty, crime, deteriorating housing stock, and abnormally high rates of health problems were and are common. At the time of Joe's assignment there, these problems were already well established. As one of the poorest areas of the city, it had attracted the most recent economically disadvantaged minority population, the Latinos. The church and attached residence fit perfectly into the generally bleak environment. The living quarters, at least Joe's, were dark, gloomy, and cold in the winter. For me they were depressing even to visit. However, none of his residential settings was anywhere near bright and cheerful. Those situations, combined with his choice to champion causes more often than not unwinnable, probably accounted for my enduring amazement at his capacity not only to carry on but to do so with cheerfulness and enthusiasm.

Joe's relationship with the pastor was superficially cordial but remained distant. But characteristically, Joe became very close to the housekeeper, Rose Lunetta, and her family. His relationship with the pastor appeared strained from the outset, which was no surprise given that the assignment was a disciplinary move for Joe and a penance for the Monsignor. But, for a time, Joe was able to make the best of the situation, taking the initiative to become acquainted with the community through personal (and usually unannounced) visits to the homes of his parishioners as well as other residents. I remember my amazement when he told me about strolling through the neighborhood and randomly stopping at homes to introduce himself. It struck me as highly unusual, especially in a poor inner-city area. I would visualize this big red-headed guy in a Roman collar wandering about ringing doorbells. But it worked. Maybe it was the shock effect, but most residents responded warmly to his openness and spontaneity. He became very well liked by the parishioners and other residents, who were happily unaware that, from the Bishop's perspective, his presence there was an exile to a gulag.

In addition to acquainting himself with neighbors and parishioners, Joe became actively involved with the parish grammar school, where he also was well liked and respected by the nuns and students. But the growing popularity of this outcast was not welcomed by the pastor. He was generally civil to Joe but maintained his pastoral authority and distance. He may have seen Joe as a threat to his position as number one. While he never actually said so, it was evident from Joe's stories of parish life that their relationship was guarded. Joe was also uncomfortable with the pastor's excessive attention to the altar boys, an attention that included trips with them to New York City. This was well before the late 1990s when the American priesthood became notorious for attracting and/or nurturing men with socially unacceptable sexual preferences, pedophilia prominent among them. Joe made no direct allegations of this, nor was there any hint in our conversations that he suspected active sexual contacts. Joe clearly disapproved, but more in the form of disappointment than concern for the safety of the boys. In the context or his demonstrated advocacy for the exploited, it is difficult to believe he could have ignored active pedophilia had he known or even suspected, and in that time, before victims were speaking out, it was truly unthinkable. Given my own skepticism about the bases for the "vocations" of several of Joe's seminary classmates, his concern about that behavior only fueled my prejudice. But while I considered the behavior grossly inappropriate, I never thought the impulses could have been acted upon without alarms sounding. Joe described his boss' behavior as a "personality disorder." Only in hindsight do I wonder if he might have missed something. Still, I have no basis for concluding anything more than Joe did, nor do my conversations with the nuns who taught at the parish school suggest other than inappropriate behavior. It may well have been no more than a symptom of what some observers see as inevitable abnormalities in many aging celibate prelates. Moreover, the aggressive investigations in recent years would very likely have brought to light any overt illicit behavior.

Fortunately and characteristically, as Joe was developing a strong friendship with Rose Lunetta's family, they in turn had begun the process of adopting our mother who lived alone for many years in the Marine Drive apartments. Rose's own family at the time consisted of her aging father, two sisters, and their children, all of whom lived on West Delevan Avenue. Among their family routines was serving pasta fagioli at least once a week, principally to please the father. Rose always made extra, which she would bring to Joe for delivery to Gramma. (Around that time, the name for mom or ma in our and my sister's house, became Gramma, the name we all picked up from our children.) There it joined other leftovers from the kitchens of Rose, the rectory, and Gramma — all neatly wrapped in foil and stacked in Gramma's freezer. More often than not, the pasta fagioli migrated to my house where it was relished far more by me than by Gramma. We often wondered if Gramma ever had to provide staples for herself because of the constant supply of leftovers from Rose. Joe also began around this time to do most of the shopping for Gramma, a practice that continued till his death and in a way contributed to it. One of Gramma's favorite quick meals was canned chop suey. When Joe was killed, the first blow was to the top of his head with one of those cans from among the groceries he had just purchased but not yet delivered to Gramma.

Joe's reputation as a soft touch was continuing its development during his tenure at Immaculate Conception. His used car of the time was terminal and he paid $400 to Ann and me for her Corvair. Unfortunately, but typically, its useful, or at least trouble-free, life was nearly over. One of his parishioners, however, was worse off, having seen his only means of transportation give up the ghost. He offered Joe $200 for the Corvair, claiming to have the skill to keep it running. The deal was consummated with a $20 "down payment" that turned out to be the only payment. I remember standing one morning with Joe on the church steps when this gentleman walked by on the other side of the street. The encounter was a friendly greeting by both men as though nothing had ever happened. This was long after both Joe and I knew the $20 was payment in full. Astonished by the casualness

The author Ray Bissonette (at left in second row) enjoys a family gathering with brother Joe, sister Joanne and "Gramma," 1980.

of the greeting, I turned to Joe asking if that wasn't the guy who owed him nearly $200. Joe said it was but he was having money problems and nothing much could be done. That incident always reminded me of Joe's values about money that were so much at odds with mine and most people's. He was careful about other people's property but had little interest in accumulating money or much of anything. About the only thing I remember being a priority for him was saving regularly for his next very used car. Curiously, despite this attitude and his generosity with whatever he had, he abhorred waste. While he would spend readily on others, he would live on air whenever possible. I think we all learned that by growing up in a home where bread crusts were saved and paper bags, wax paper, and the occasional luxurious foil were used many times before being retired. Having been born in the depths of the depression, Joe may have learned those lessons sooner and better.

The used car incident, however, was only a minor reprise of his first and largest "unsecured loan." One of his parishioners at St. Joseph's in North Tonawanda had become friendly with Joe during his time there. He was a builder who was in "temporary" financial difficulty back in the early 1960s. He told Joe he needed $5000 to prevent the loss of his business. Joe borrowed the money from my mother for whom it was the lion's share of her life savings. Of course the loan was not repaid, but Joe replaced Gramma's money in tiny installments over years until it was fully repaid. To put this in perspective, at that time newly graduating Ph.D.s from the University of Maryland where I was studying were accepting teaching jobs where that was the annual salary. I know the man who borrowed the money and never once heard Joe speak ill of him, despite the huge burden that loan placed on Joe for years. In fact, Joe continued to have dinner at the home of him and his wife well into the period when Joe was repaying Gramma out of his own very shallow pocket. Thinking we were witnessing an error in judgment by an idealistic and gullible young priest, we were, in fact, watching the playing out of a personal value system in which accumulation of things counted for little beyond keeping one from being a problem for someone else. Using a distinction I find useful, Joe could be described as foolish but not stupid. To the extent this was a shortcoming or failure of judgment, it was by choice not default. His foolishness was a conscious decision that led him to live out the belief held by many and practiced by few that one truly owns only what is given away.

Remarkably, nearly 15 years after his death, I was reminded pointedly of this. On Christmas Eve, 2001, I received a phone call from someone looking for Father Bissonette's brother. He had found me in the phone book after calling several relatives. He needed a ride from Cheektowaga to the lower west side to deliver some food and gifts to some family whose relationship to him wasn't at all clear to me. We were in the midst of one of Buffalo's legendary snowstorms, then in the process of dropping over seven feet of snow in one week. The caller, "Mark," told me Joe had once done him a favor, and when asked how he could be repaid, told Mark to "pass it on." Mark remembered that and opined that it was his unselfishness that got him killed. Mark was obviously disturbed in some way, but I found myself challenged to take on the sucker role Joe played so well. I couldn't go then but did early Christmas afternoon, by which time Mark was on the west side and needed a ride home. It was a difficult and frustrating trip. I got to the lower west side address given to me by Mark's father to find it didn't exist. After knocking on nearly every door on the street and talking with several residents, I finally approached for the second time a man who was digging his car out of the snow.

In retrospect, his advice was amusing and very sensible. Responding to my obvious frustration he asked me in a very matter of fact way if I had checked both blocks around the address I had shown him saying, "You looked up there; you looked down there and didn't find him?" After a pause for my affirmative answer, he said, "Then go home." Later that day I found that Mark's father had transposed the numbers, and I had been searching in the wrong blocks. I also learned, with the help of one of my Christmas dinner guests, why the man in the street was so unsympathetic — he thought I was on a drug buy.

Like so many of Joe's adventures and misadventures, it seemed a waste of time. While I expected that before I went, I also knew I was being reminded of how things often turn out in the course of placing the well being of others before one's own and dismissing all considerations of convenience and prudence. Probably a Christmas Eve distress call during a snowstorm from someone looking for the closest thing he could get to Joe moved me to attempt an imitation. But the imitation failed when I told my friends and family: Joe would simply have done it and none but Mark, his father, Joe, and maybe one other would ever know.

CHAPTER TWELVE

THE HAPPY WARRIOR

Perhaps it's no coincidence that Joe chose to write his history master's thesis on Al Smith, known widely as the happy warrior. Joe too, in lifelong contradiction to our father's fear that he was too timid to manage in this harsh world, was never the plaster saint that the circumstances of his life and death could easily suggest. While he died from exsanguination, in life he was never the austere bloodless martyr.

At an event honoring him posthumously, I recall struggling to think how best to capture his person and history in a few minutes. When I took my turn at the podium I remarked about how mystified I had always been that he maintained such an upbeat attitude when his life and work were always into the wind and replete with frustration and setbacks. My explanation was the support he received from so many like-minded colleagues whose identity and even existence I began to know only after his death. I thought then it was a fair guess but now believe it was merely a partial explanation. To a large extent, Joe's positive attitude was attributable to his reluctance to display his emotions. His happy times were apparent enough, but their reasons had to be inferred, especially if they were the result of some personal accomplishment. Those you learned about, if at all, from others. For example, our family learned about his election to senior class president at Canisius College from a notice in the newspaper.

Similarly, the bad news and hard times were rarely expressed openly. He was, for the most part, not pretending the enthusiasm and optimism for which he is remembered, but beneath the "happy warrior" impression was his fair share of discouragement, resentment, anger, and cynicism. Indeed, I am convinced that he recognized disproportionate levels of comfort and self-satisfaction as not only self-deceptive but symptoms of moral sloth. Again I am reminded of his slight but revealing modification of the liturgy where he changed the petition about protection from anxiety from *all* to *needless*. I have only heard one other priest make that change. It was in the winter of 1999, when Father Bob Perelli said one of the Masses at St. Joseph's in north Buffalo. After Mass I approached him and we talked about that little similarity and my interpretation of it. He seemed in agreement with my view of it and was not surprised that Joe had done the same. Interestingly,

Perelli's regular ministry is providing services for AIDS patients and their families. He understands walking into the wind.

But not all the warfare was happy. While at Immaculate Conception, Joe had a supply of literature intended for use in conjunction with a demonstration, probably opposing the Vietnamese war. He had stored it in a hallway in the rectory and when he went to find it, discovered it was missing. He asked Monsignor Harrington if he knew anything about it and was told it had been thrown out because of its inappropriate message. Joe was stunned and furious, and after some words from Harrington about Joe's unseemly involvement with things other than sacramental, Joe asked, "Are you going to the Bishop or am I?" This flare-up marked the end of his tenure at Immaculate. Shortly after, he packed his belongings and went to his mother's apartment to conduct his search for his next assignment. He remained there for approximately six weeks. He was actively exploring options but no one seems to know where he spent his days. Each morning he would leave her apartment and return for dinner as though maintaining a regular work schedule. While I knew he was between acts, I had no idea that he had no income. This would have been acutely painful for Joe, in that he always felt a strong obligation to pull his weight, and the idea of "sponging" off my mother, who herself, lived on a shoestring, would have stung. Adding to his frustration was the fact that an opening existed at St. Brigid's, an inner city parish in the Perry projects whose pastor, Bob Sweeny, was looking for an associate and would have welcomed Joe readily. Frequently during his assignment with Harrington he had expressed to me and to the Diocese a strong interest in joining Sweeny, a liberal priest known for his intelligence and courageous activism. Like Immaculate Conception, it was a poor inner-city parish, but an assignment there would have involved working with another activist priest whom Joe knew and respected. But the Bishop was not about to make it too simple. Joe would first be appropriately chastened and neither he nor anyone would be given to believe that his pattern of placing service before obedience to authority was to be rewarded. So he waited, 15 years ordained and back home with his mother, until the assignment to Brigid's could appear to be an initiative of the Diocese rather than an acquiescence to either Sweeny or Joe.

During the early 1970s, he and I would often play squash at the Canisius College Athletic Center at Main and Delevan. Sometimes we would retire afterward to The Locker Room, a bar at Delevan and Delaware, for a couple beers. One night he told me of his dream of leading a diocese-wide program for services to youth, but he was uncertain of the hierarchy's receptivity to the idea. His uncertainty was well founded. Nothing ever came of it, nor do I know what steps he took or had taken to sell the idea. Many years later, in reviewing his job preference form completed in October 1980, I learned that youth work was only a moderately attractive ministry for him and, interestingly, given his years at Turner High School, secondary education was listed as barely acceptable; which may well explain the recollections of several students that Joe seemed often distracted while at Turner. Recurring top choices were inner city, social justice, liturgy, counseling, religious education, and work with adults. One wonders if his experience as an educator, which was highly successful according to the testimony of former students and colleagues, was suffered in silence, or if his forced removal from that role embittered him. In any case, the grand plan he confided in me in the early 1970s was clearly not apparent in his ministry preferences in 1980.

Other puzzling entries on the preference list were his choices under the category "other." On a seven-point scale, Latin America was listed near the bottom at number six. This questionnaire was completed only a couple years before the murder in El Salvador of Archbishop Oscar Romero and Joe's leadership in establishing a special memorial mass and dinner. Romero is widely remembered for his outspoken advocacy for the poor in Central America, especially in El Salvador where the United States was supporting a ruthless dictatorship presumably to stop the spread of communism from Honduras. One suspects, as Joe did, that communism was at least as much a threat to American economic interests in Latin America as it was to the ideal of democracy, an ideal remaining to this day an elusive reality in that part of the world. At the 19th annual Central American Dinner, now called the Joe Bissonette Central American Dinner, held on March 23, 2000, one of Joe's statements from the early 1980s is quoted in the program: "Our policy in Central America is so contrary to the message of the prophets of the kingdom, we seem to be exalting the oppressive princes and pulling down the lowly." The wording of the statement is very significant in any recollection of Joe. It is easy to think of him as having become caught up in social causes to the detriment of his ecclesiastical vocation, but here, and throughout his life, the struggle for social justice is clearly derived from the life and teachings of Christ and his disciples. Quite contrary to the appearance of an idealistic young priest turned renegade, his priesthood evolved but his commitments remained much what they were from the outset: study and live the message of the Gospel. In that context it is no surprise that he antagonized those in positions of hierarchical authority who dined at the tables of the keepers of the kingdom. Christ was crucified for it and Joe, for much of his priesthood, was ignored when possible or muzzled through various administrative tactics.

It appears that Joe's years at Immaculate Conception marked the solidification of his commitment to social activism. While there, its centrality to his priesthood began to take concrete form as his definition of his vocation fully embraced advocacy for his parishioners as well as others without an audible voice. While the assignment at Immaculate may have been culminative, his identification by others and himself as an advocate was evident far earlier. Indeed, he was at Immaculate in the first place for convincing the Bishop that he was poisoning young minds at Turner by insisting on living the Gospel rather than focusing on its sacramental embellishments.

Jim Mang, for many years the director of the Western New York Peace Center, was in the priesthood until 1977, having been ordained about four years after Joe. Even more outspoken than

Joe addressing a Peace and Justice Symposium , ca. 1984.

Joe, he was personally warned by the Bishop "to cease and desist all activities leading to the downfall of the United States government." Mang remembered Joe both during and before his time at Immaculate as a more senior priest with whom he could easily discuss his activist ideals and find not only a sympathetic ear but also an affirmation that such a calling was appropriate and necessary to the priesthood. Right after Joe's murder, Jim's impressions of Joe were expressed in a letter published in *The Buffalo News* on March 17, 1987.

> From the first day I met Fr. Joe Bissonette ... I knew there was something special about this man ... a Catholic priest unequalled in depth of faith, compassion for people, dedication to the call for peace and justice, and commitment to the radical call of the Gospel .... The reason I attended Mass at St. Bart's over the last couple years was because of

> Father Bissonette who never gave a sermon separate from himself, the community, and the world... [he] had a dream of a better world — a dream he lived every day of his life. Though we are angry, frustrated, and saddened by his death, we dare not let his dream fade.

Immediately upon his arrival at Immaculate there was evidence that Joe's role would extend well beyond the altar. I remember again Joe's description of his strolls through the parish neighborhood, mainly Allentown, knocking on the doors of residents, Catholic or not, to get a feel for the community and meet the people. I also remember thinking that as somewhat assertive, or at least unusual, for any priest, especially Joe, whom I still regarded as basically shy. But again, I was missing the distinction between his personal comfort level and how he perceived and performed his role as a priest. Among the residents who remembers his activism in the Allentown community is Carole Holcberg, a former social worker and now proprietor of a successful real estate agency.

During the latter years of Joe's tenure at Immaculate, Carole was director of the Allentown Association. In the late 1960s, the Department of Housing and Urban Development (HUD) had begun a program to rehabilitate urban housing stock. Qualifying owners could obtain low interest rehabilitation loans and many Allentown properties qualified. Administration of the program, however, lay with the city administration, under the authority of an individual Carole describes simply as incompetent. The mishandling of this potentially vital project led to intense resentment and frustration among many in the Immaculate parish area. Along with a local Native American citizen activist, Geraldine Memmo, Joe started an organization called Association of Citizens To Improve Our Neighborhood (ACTION). Formed specifically in response to the city's bungling of the HUD program, leadership in this group not only placed Joe visibly and centrally in a community leadership role, it shifted his political adversaries from the leadership of the Church to secular officials.

But this was not an all-consuming role. He still maintained his principal focus on integrating the parish with the surrounding community. Among his accomplishments in that area was including a folk Mass in the weekend liturgy that already had a Spanish Mass. Observers, however, point to his personal example more than programmatic changes as effecting the integration. For example, Carole Holcberg emphasizes that Joe was in the neighborhoods constantly and rarely in a Roman collar. His genuine concern for the community and its individual families, combined with his unwavering sense of humor, were the qualities that drew people to him and the parish.

However, the political action was neither diminished nor mitigated by these gentler qualities. Joe's intolerance of the ineptitude of the City in allowing the HUD program to do its job was unwavering. Still, he managed to keep his anger under control, approaching his dealings with City Hall in a style that was quiet, measured, but relentless. When Joe left the parish, ACTION was incorporated into the Allentown Association.

Bill Stanton's favorite "gentle giant" snapshot— Joe feeding a fawn, ca. 1980.

CHAPTER THIRTEEN

THOSE BASTARDS

Joe's frustrations and anger were not always expressed in measured, controlled behavior. While earlier noting the interesting choice of Al Smith for his history master's thesis, I may have projected an image of a cheerful Paul Bunyan gleefully hacking away at the forests of oppression. While the sense of humor and upbeat personality were real enough, the happy warrior analogy must be seen in the context of a man whose readily aroused feelings certainly included and displayed anger. As long as I knew him, Joe was exquisitely sensitive to those he saw as unfairly treated, especially the weak and helpless. Because of this sensitivity, he was proportionately infuriated by those who ignored them, denied them, or overtly exploited them. For those, often the keepers of the keys in business or politics, Joe was capable of virulent anger. "Those bastards!" was an expression others and I well remember hearing him use when referring to people in power who profited from the misery of others. Usually "the bastards" were not individuals but political or corporate entities, but he could and did direct that anger at individuals on occasion, usually local or national political leaders who, in his view, defaulted on their responsibility to represent their constituents fairly. One occasion I remember well because it so surprised me. He was fulminating about the guest speaker at a Canisius College *Di Gamma* dinner we had attended together. *Di Gamma* was the college honor society and the annual black tie dinner was and continues to be a well-attended event with long cocktail hours and copious supplies of booze. Joe and I both honored the tradition by having at least our share and probably a bit more. The speaker, the superintendent of the Lancaster Schools, had delivered an appropriately articulate and high-minded speech that reminded the audience of their special place of privilege in the world. On the way home, Joe began a jeremiad about the speaker's quotations of John D. Rockefeller and other captains of industry who had made their fortunes on the backs of the poor and ignorant. Certainly his tongue was as loose as my mind was dull, but I have always remembered that anger. Both its openness and intensity caught me by surprise.

Anger and resentment were understandably constant companions of someone whose life was devoted to the marginal. I also recall my astonishment when he related an incident of standing on a coffee table at a cocktail party to excoriate the guests for their insensitivity to the racially and economically oppressed. Regrettably, I cannot remember the specifics of the incident, only the incomprehensible image of my big, respected, and always-respectful brother haranguing polite company from a coffee table. At the time I was inclined to attribute the incident more to the cocktails than the table, especially when recalled along with the rant following the *DiGamma* dinner. Although those isolated incidents reflect some loss of self-discipline, they do remind me that he was never far from the edge of rage any more than he was ever far from what prompted it. But while he was certainly spurred by anger, it did not consume him. For the most part, he was cheerful and positive, reserving most of his anger for perceived abuses of power and exploitation of those without it. However, the definition of abuse of power easily and naturally extended to the arbitrary exercise of authority, especially where he saw privilege and rank trumping respect for those with neither. The incident of his refusal to return to the seminary during a break to perform for a visiting potentate stands for me as a classic case.

Nor was his capacity for anger limited to official misconduct. In the winter the collar of his raincoat was put to good use in the car. He would quickly flip the collar up to conceal his Roman collar when he found it necessary to roll down the window to offer some advice on driving skills to another motorist. After his first year in the seminary, while he was working in a summer program for young people in one of the rural parishes, an incident occurred that not only aroused his anger but haunted him for years to come. He was first to come upon an accident scene in which one of his colleagues had crashed into a culvert after being forced off the road by a reckless driver who drove off. As I recall, there were serious injuries to the young people, perhaps even a fatality. Joe was wild, openly wishing he'd arrived sooner and been able to chase down and catch the "bastard." I have no doubt that he would have tried.

His proclivity to paste the "bastard" label was part of a broader tendency to be rather easily roused to the side of a cause he thought worthy, sometimes shooting from the hip in the process. In a larger context, one of Joe's enduring and sometimes endearing characteristics was a naïveté that bordered on an almost childlike simplicity in several areas of his life. His loan of our mother's money to a parishioner was a typical behavior. Another special area of innocence concerned women. While not generically ignorant, he was virtually blind to their frequent attraction to him. Although he would often note how some women seemed to find priests an attractive target for flirtation either out of a sense of special challenge or a feeling of safety because of the celibacy vow. He also was very aware of the risks of mixing women with booze and was fond of saying, "You get a couple beers under your belt and you want a woman under your arm." One summer when I was a teenager, I accompanied some of his seminarian friends to the Erie County Fair. While there, we wandered into the side show area and came upon a strip show being pitched to the passers-by with a couple of jaded but well-endowed ladies listlessly writhing on the platform. When I later told Joe about the experience, he asked if the group I was with had walked away or stood around. The answer was the latter. All I recall of Joe's response was a silent but knowing nod of the head. Of course this occurred during his early years of unqualified and enthusiastic embrace of the dictates of his new calling.

But to find himself the object of a woman's affection was a different story. Here the ingenuousness was impenetrable. During his time at Immaculate, he spent much of his off duty time with the nuns who ran the school. Among other things, they were a source of companionship and, perhaps, equally importantly, meals. They still laugh when recalling his frequent inquiries about whether they were "going to eat tonight." That not so ingenuous inquiry always resulted in the desired invitation. He was the perfect dinner guest; hungry but indiscriminant, very grateful, and present for duty when it was time to wash the dishes. As this camaraderie developed, he failed to see a concurrent development — in one of the younger nuns, an affection for Joe that far exceeded any spiritual or professional dimensions and was transparent to everyone but Joe. As Sisters Patrice Ryan and Gail Glenn put it, "She was throwing herself at him." Eventually it reached a point where Gail, then the school principal, met with Joe to apprise him of the obvious. Joe, as she remembers, was dumbfounded but did adjust his behavior to avoid encouraging the attraction.

Ignorance of his attractiveness to women probably accounted for his playfulness with those he knew and doubtless added to his appeal. Gail also recalls the summer evenings during the pastor's absence when Joe would "borrow" his large Buick and take off with some of the nuns to a drive-in movie.

My own wife, Ann, had developed a deep affection for Joe. Among other things, she profoundly respected his integrity, generosity, and personal warmth. I think also, her own overriding commitment to her role as a parent found a kindred spirit in Joe, whose love for his nieces and nephews was indistinguishable from that of a father. Certainly her affection for Joe was indistinguishable from her feelings for any blood relatives. She would herself readily acknowledge that. An incident in the late 1980s, shortly after his murder, always serves to remind me of her love for him. We were watching *Hill Street Blues* on television. In this particular episode, one of the principal characters had been wounded gravely and his fellow cops were waiting anxiously outside the intensive care unit, until, with great relief, they learned he was out of danger. As I watched, I looked across the room to see that Ann had tears in her eyes. I knew the reason and it was confirmed when I asked her what was wrong. We both were reminded of Joe's attack and wishing it could have had a similar outcome. Joe's relationship with our family and my sister's certainly explained my single major disappointment with the path chosen by my big brother: he took himself out of the gene pool.

Joe's hair trigger reaction to certain people and situations had a paradoxical quality. He could be stymied by an inability to come down firmly on one side or another where an issue he studied was freighted with evidence and arguments pointing in opposite directions. During one of his homilies at St. Bartholomew's, he told the congregation of the impatience of some of his older colleagues in the priesthood with his ambivalence on certain religious and secular issues. They had tried to make him understand that members of the flock expected and deserved clear guidance from their clergy. But, as Joe pointed out, clear, unequivocal positions were not only seldom possible in complex human issues but often intellectually dishonest. He was very clear about that.

Not surprisingly, such indecisiveness was equally problematic in the political domain. In 1979, Joe accepted an invitation from John LaFalce, a member of Congress and friend of mine for many years, to do an internship in the House of Representatives. I was in D.C. toward the end of the ten-week internship, and over dinner, John and I discussed his experience with Joe. John was exasperated with Joe's inability to present him with a clear position on certain issues he had researched. At the restaurant, John described this as "doctrinaire ambivalence," a term he tried to retrieve almost before it left his lips. I didn't take personal offense, but have often thought of how frustrating this must have been for both of them — John needing to articulate a position and Joe needing to be true to the facts as he could find and interpret them. Perhaps exacerbating that situation was the issue of the mandatory military draft law that was being debated in the face of its imminent expiration. Joe would be inclined to find the competing arguments more readily than the single position.

While questioning Joe's alacrity in jumping on bandwagons well before he knew the whole story, I was often guilty of shooting from the hip about him. I was certain, for example, that his vehemence about United States policy in Central America during the 1970s and 1980s was somewhat extreme. I also saw a number of indications of skepticism on the part of Jack Weimer, who probably knew him as well as anyone. Yet after Joe's death, documents released by our government essentially vindicated Joe's conviction that we were actively and vigorously supporting oppression of democracy and human rights in order to support regimes friendly to our national interests, even when those "national" interests were indistinguishable from the interests of corporations with powerful lobbies.

The seeming paradox of Joe's early leap to judgment on social issues is tempered by his subsequent reserve once he studied and found the competing facts in many situations. Still, his life remained a delicate balance, occasionally tipped, between toleration and attack. Not surprisingly, a solid dedication to peace could not always be peacefully expressed. The ambivalence noticed by LaFalce and others was often the harder course when the easier path was to edit the reality and form an expedient judgment. In some respects it reminds me of Chesterton's observation that standing firm in the face of racing change could require more strength than leading the charge. The fire and ice coexistence in Joe of gentleness and strength, along with other apparent dualities, was expressed by Ned Cuddy, a history professor at Daemen College. His words, written shortly after Joe's death, explain much of what this narrative struggles to express:

Something gentle and beautiful seeped out of the life of our community when the killer's knife took Father Bissonette from us. Joe's days in our midst seem all the more precious against the stark background of his tragic death. Those of us who were fortunate enough to have worked with him will long be inspired by lingering memories of this dedicated priest. We will remember his deep, authentic spirituality; his detachment from material goods, surpassed only by his generosity to those in need; his gentle ways which concealed a backbone of steel; his courageous dedication to peace and justice; his unshakeable commitment to the Church even in the face of opposition from Church authorities.

CHAPTER FOURTEEN

THE NOT SO PERFECT PARISH

Within the mix of local clergy during the tumultuous years after Vatican II was a somewhat mysterious and paradoxical figure named Bob Sweeny. Sweeny, apparently born to the purple, was left-leaning in his commitment to social activism, particularly in his opposition to racism both in the larger society and the Church. But for whatever reasons, he managed to survive during the McNulty era. Joe mentioned often his admiration for Sweeny's work and his interest in joining him in his ministry to the residents in and around the Perry Projects on Louisiana Street near South Park Avenue. To my recollection, this desire was shared by Sweeny, but not by the diocesan leaders who perhaps anticipated problems in the linking of two popular but unconventional liberal priests. As mentioned earlier, Joe had requested assignment to Sweeny's parish, St. Brigid's, but it was denied, despite a vacancy for an assistant. I remember wishing he could be assigned there, thinking it would be fulfilling and stimulating to work with a bright and respected priest who shared Joe's principal values. It would have been the first time in his then 15 years in the priesthood that he was not the black sheep in the rectory. It appeared that Joe was actually under consideration for the position but would not be granted the assignment while it was seen as an assent to his request. In many ways it was a natural for Joe. St. Brigid's was a poor and dying parish that lacked even a church. That had burned years earlier and the insurance money had gone to keep the parish alive rather than rebuild. Joe's activist inclinations could be satisfied, perhaps even overwhelmed there, without spilling into the mainstream of the Diocese.

Indeed, in 1973, Joe completed his temporary exile at his mother's apartment and joined Sweeny as the assistant pastor at St. Brigid's. I was overjoyed, seeing it as something of a victory and vindication that he was at work in the inner city for the first time as a member of a team. I knew nothing then nor do I now of how this move was seen by the Diocese, but it was surely not a reward for irritating the Bishop. Possibly they considered it a way to help a moribund parish community while at the same time keeping Joe, and Sweeny too, removed from the mainstream of the community and Diocese. What I know for sure, it was not an assignment many would consider desirable. The physical plant was ancient and in poor repair. Creature comforts for our species were spare but attractive to the rodents. I remember vividly spending an evening there shortly after Joe's arrival, trying to dampen the shrill squeaks in an old bedspring that more or less supported his mattress. I was only partially successful, but he never complained. How well he slept I can only guess, but he soon adopted the neighborhood as his own and, I believe, found the work satisfying and rewarding.

But the great expectations of the Bissonette-Sweeny team shaking the trees in the Western New York Diocese remained mostly expectations. Perhaps they were fantasy to begin with or, as my current hypothesis runs, Sweeny's fire was burning down. Joe was never critical of him, but neither were there any reports consistent with the picture Joe had painted when initially seeking the assignment. For whatever reasons, Joe's tenure there was concurrent with Sweeny's progressive disengagement with the parish. Those close to the siuation at the time tell me that Sweeny was rarely there, spending most of his time at his home in Canada. It would have been very characteristic of Joe never to mention this to me or anyone. And his silence on the subject would fit perfectly with his very careful handling of personal information that could be embarrassing or stigmatizing. What happened is unclear, but Sweeny's flame appeared to have guttered.

Much of Joe's time at Brigid's was spent with parishioners and others living in the nearby Commodore Perry housing projects, then and now, crowded and dangerous public housing inhabited mostly by minorities. Typical of these projects nationally, they began as well-intentioned solutions to unavailable and unaffordable housing for the poor, only to become "reservations" where squatters were prevalent and gangs financed by the drug trade ruled. For those seeking decent, affordable housing it was a tough and hazardous world.

Very telling about Joe's work at Brigid's and elsewhere is the story, alluded to earlier, Ann and I heard after a memorial service following his death. The woman who approached us told us that Joe had been a surrogate father to her sons. Her life was a struggle against the odds: her oldest boy was serving a long sentence for manslaughter and the others were at risk of the same, especially in the absence of a male adult in the household. In her view, Joe's attention to her other children was responsible not only for their surviving the ghetto, but also escaping and succeeding because of his supervision, encouragement, and availability as an adult male role model.

That brief encounter was the beginning of my education about my brother's invisible life. Until his death I had always wondered why his priesthood so consumed his time. Whenever he was at our home or my mother's he seemed to be just arriving from or leaving for some meeting or other commitment. Frankly, I often wondered whether much of that activity was busywork done out of a sense of obligation to make appearances at everybody's project of the day. It would have been like Joe to do that. And I suspected that he maybe was being eaten up by an excess of these obligations that were of questionable value in my assessment. He was nearly incapable of saying no to anyone and totally incapable of defaulting on a commitment once made. Everything I saw was consistent with the belief that he might have been spinning his wheels with too many projects with too few chances of ever getting past the talk stage. But I later learned that, even where that might have been the case from an objective analysis, the presence of the big guy in the Roman collar was important anyway. His support, and often leadership, offered hope and comfort to people who were used to very little of either. And, in addition to the incessant meetings, there were those even less visible hours he spent in hospital rooms, holding centers, homes, and apartments, where human problems and tragedies were played out in the presence of someone who was special to the families and lent appropriate meaning and dignity to their otherwise back page stories.

Following his death, this reality became so very clear. People would approach us with stories of how Joe was there when junior was arrested, grandpa was dying, or dad lost his job. The stories went on, and the seven-day weeks became understandable. Sixteen years after his death and four years after beginning this memoir, I discovered an old Sunday bulletin from St. Brigid's that confirmed all of the impressions related here. It was from September 2, 1979, his final Sunday there and just before he and I left for Washington, D.C. for his internship with LaFalce. (In fact, written in his hand on the bulletin is the address of where he would live during that month in D.C.) I don't know the author, but the message, entitled "Who is Father Joe?" is as follows:

How can a few printed words express who Father Joe Bissonette has been for each of us here at St. Brigid's during the past six and one-half years? Can a few words tell about Father Joe, the always available neighbor who simply did whatever was needed whenever it was needed, whether that need involved visiting the sick and shut ins, providing comfort and advice for those in trouble, supporting and encouraging the imprisoned, distributing surplus food, running errands, shoveling snow, or buying ice cream? Or should the words tell about Father Joe, the patient and supportive listener at countless parish and community meetings? Or Father Joe, the priest who brought a spirit of prayer and care to the liturgy, who always carefully prepared the words he spoke to us in his homilies, even when he knew only three or four of us would be gathered daily to hear the Word? Or Father Joe, the faithful teacher, both of children and adults? Or Father Joe who always seemed to turn up in the Primary School when they were making peanut butter?

Or Father Joe, the welcome guest, every cook's delight, who came to the table with indiscriminate taste buds no matter whether it was his third or fourth meal? Or Father Joe, the man who lived out his concern for social justice by being the just man among us, speaking the hard but truthful word when needed, yet serving all, of whatever race or creed with equal gentleness and concern?

All these words express a part of who he was for us: neighbor, listener, priest, teacher, cartoonist, guest, celebrator, just man. But if only one word could describe him, the word is CHRISTIAN. Because of his presence among us as a Christian,

> we here at St. Brigid's will never dare to claim we do not know who Jesus is. We will never be able to say we do not know the meaning of living the Christian life. We have been privileged to have among us a living Word — an authentic, honest-to-goodness walking, talking, praying, laughing, living man of God and the Gospel. And above all else, Father Joe has shown us by the way he lives among us, who it is that we as Christians are called to be. Such authentic Christianity is always a challenge and always misinterpreted by those who do not see the source of such living. But we have seen this life daily. Our greatest thank you for the gift of Father Joe is to assure him that we too will try to live the Christian life, form the Christian community he has helped create among us. In our sadness at his departure, we turn to the Faith he has nurtured among us that tells us that friends, sisters, and brothers in the Lord are never really absent from each other. Though Father Joe will no longer be our shepherd, he will always be our friend and brother in the Lord. We bless you Father Joe with thankful hearts and know that wherever you go, you will walk with the Lord and we will walk with you.

Subsequently, I learned that the time at Brigid's was especially intense with respect to community ministry. According to Sister Eileen O'Connor, a colleague and friend of Joe's, many parishioners at Brigid's were very needy and looked to the parish as a major source of help. That, combined with Joe's compulsion to help everyone he could, made this a particularly demanding assignment for him. But, instead of turning him away from his openness to the importunate needy, it set a pattern that would characterize and finally end his priesthood.

Later, when my own family suffered illness and death, I became even more appreciative of what he did for all those people. In my experience, too many of the clergy had slept through their lessons on the corporal works of mercy, and, by comparison to Joe, were weak or defaulting on significant dimensions of their priesthood. Uncomfortable in the trenches of human need, they found refuge in ritual and other trappings of their priestly roles.

Whatever may have happened between Joe and Sweeny, we do know that after five years there as Sweeny's assistant, Joe either wanted to leave Brigid's and/or thought it was time for his own pastorate. In a letter dated October 8, 1977, Joe wrote to Father Rupert Wright, the coordinator of the Diocesan Personnel Board, expressing his views on moving on, possibly to St. Martin's where the pastorate was open. While I knew nothing of the letter at the time, I recall talking with Joe about a lunch meeting with the departing pastor there that ended with a mutual understanding that the parish was not the place for a liberal activist priest. So the tour of duty at St. Brigid's continued. However, within the year, 1977, Joe became the administrator. Presumably, Sweeny, who had served in that role, departed, but I have no idea where he went, except that I heard nothing more about him from Joe or anyone — another piece in the puzzle that Joe kept to himself.

By 1979, Joe's time at St. Brigid's was over and the search that prompted the letter to Wright was now more pressing. Lacking a clear option, he took the opportunity to spend ten weeks as an intern with John LaFalce's congressional office in Washington, D.C. I, and others at the time, thought this would be a great experience and break from the routine. But for Joe it was a period of mounting anxiety. The diary he kept during that period reveals his uneasiness about where he would go and what he would do upon his return. This, combined with a growing uncertainty (one that I knew to be well founded) about his usefulness to LaFalce, appeared frequently in his notes. But still the resilience that seemed to insulate him from discouragement in his battles for the underdog was also present throughout his reflections on the experience.

The diary is remarkable in its concise but revealing snapshot of his enthusiasm for taking in new experiences and knowledge. On each left page he drew cartoon representations of his daily activities and the opposite page contained the corresponding verbal description. Each entry ended with a note about how he was feeling. Most often it was a positive "good" but often qualified. On the tenth of November he had gone to Laurel, Maryland, to visit his friend, Peter Ladley. While entering a restaurant, he stepped on a beetle. His entry that night was: "filled with excitement of good visit except for bug killing and Peter's remark that "I live with Jesuits and not Franciscans." An entry both amusing and revealing about a man never far from the simple realities of life was about having managed to iron a shirt on the same day he was beginning to sense a lack of purpose in his work. The entry: "Feeling: Still a bit uneasy about my contribution to JJL's office. Felt good about ironing the shirt." As the time passed, his qualifiers reflecting apprehension about returning home and concern about the usefulness of his work were more frequent.

When he returned from Washington and left St. Brigid's, he had been ordained 20 years, and despite the characteristic uncertainty about his contribution to JJL or anyone, his impact on those in his orbit had become very clear to them. The central elements of those impressions stand out in sharp relief against a mottled background of multiple assignments and relationships.

Mass celebrating the start of the 75th anniversary year of St. Bartholomew's Parish, February 1, 1987.

CHAPTER FIFTEEN

AS OTHERS SAW HIM

An immense consequence, predictable only in hindsight, of the myriad effects of Vatican II and the pervasive cultural upheaval of the 1960s was a virtual evacuation of the inhabitants of convents and traditional residences of religious orders. With the secularization and shrinkage of the parochial schools and other religious institutions, large numbers of nuns found themselves living in communities, usually in groups, and gradually involved in secular employment. While this took many forms, it often was in roles extending their inclination toward and preparation for community service. This type of work typically included a significant voluntary involvement. For Joe and other priests similarly engaged in community work, it was inevitable that their relationship with women religious would increase and change. Having chosen the community as his principal pulpit, Joe was among those priests brought into extensive contact with religious women who were fast becoming ubiquitous in social action programs. One result was that many of the sources for a retrospective of his life are current or former women religious; but whatever the source, the impressions of his personal traits and interpretation of his role as a priest are strikingly consistent.

During the time Joe was at Brigid's, he became active in an organization known as the Center For Justice. The Center was founded in 1972 by a coalition of area nuns from several orders who sought to focus their work toward peace initiatives, non-violence, economic equity, nuclear disarmament, and gender parity. Given Joe's values, it was a natural environment for him as well. In the view of every female acquaintance interviewed for this memoir, Joe had already distinguished himself as "factory equipped" on the issue of gender parity. They found, to their instant pleasure, a priest to whom gender distinctions regarding personal or professional stature were simply non-existent. Unlike other issues where he engaged in conscious and often difficult reflection and effort, the treatment of females as equal seemed entirely natural. From women, religious and lay, the stories of Joe's helping in the kitchen and washing dishes seem endless and consistent with my own memory of Joe at family meals beating everyone to the sink after dinner.

Bonny Butler, then a sister of St. Mary of Namur, first met Joe following completion of her master's studies in theology at Fordham University. It was 1983 and she had volunteered at the Center for Justice while Joe was still board chairman. Together with others, they worked intensively on developing a program of assistance to the poor in El Salvador whom they believed were being abused and exploited in the service of United States policy there. Their efforts took the form of a Medical Aid to El Salvador Committee that continues today under the name of the Latin American Solidarity Committee. Her memories of Joe resonate with others who knew and worked with him in those days. She specifically remembers his sense of humor, his comfortable manner, his lack of pretense, and his consistency in "putting his money where his mouth was and not letting others stand in the rain while he stayed dry."

Clearly, the fondness of the nuns was not always limited to professional admiration. Ann Hastee first met Joe in the 1970s while she was assigned to St. Brigid's as one of the teaching staff in the school. Admittedly in love with him, she openly describes the traits she found so compelling and in a matter-of-fact manner identifies virtually every nun who worked closely with Joe as being "in love with him." Although perhaps something of a hyperbole from someone frankly not objective, there appears to be a pattern of powerful affection and admiration among nearly every woman interviewed for this memoir. While not gainsaying Joe's likely appeal to the opposite sex, one cannot overlook a suspicion that part of his attraction may have derived from his distinction from what nuns had typically experienced in their relationship with priests. Of course the Church had two millennia of male dominated hierarchical tradition by the time of Joe and Vatican II, a circumstance that would exaggerate the appeal of a priest who washed dishes.

One of the activities that developed in the Center was sanctuary for refugees fleeing persecution in Central America. Beginning with ad hoc voluntary assistance, the help evolved into a formal program under the initial leadership of Sister Bonny who formed an organization called VIVE, now a major organization supporting refugees from throughout the world, seeking asylum in Canada. It appears that Joe's sensitization to the plight of the Central American poor, largely due to American political policy, took shape during this period. Whatever the source, it became a powerful factor in Joe's concern with structural issues in social justice and certainly marked the end to any illusions he may have had regarding American foreign policy as informed principally by democratic values.

One of the early leaders in the asylum movement in Buffalo was Sister Karen Klimczak. Karen now runs a program for early release prisoners in the building that was once Joe's home — the rectory at St. Bartholomew's. Her facility is virtually a shrine to Joe, particularly the room where he was killed. In fact, the A. Joseph Bissonette Memorial Foundation, established to carry on his work, routinely meets in that house. Karen is one of Joe's greatest fans and rarely misses an opportunity to remind people of his ministry and influence on the community. Among her most vivid memories of Joe was an offer he made when she first began her prison ministry. He told her to come to him if she ever needed help. From a man with no material possessions and zero influence in the Church hierarchy, it was a curious offer. But she took it at face value and still does. She will tell you without qualification that Joe continues to back his original offer and she relates numerous occasions when her calls for his help have been answered promptly and fully. And Karen, a diminutive woman operating a home for male convicts, is a no-nonsense administrator not given to hyperbole except where Joe is concerned.

In February 1980, Joe began what was to be his final assignment. He was named administrator of St. Bartholomew's parish. Located on Buffalo's east side across from the County Hospital, "St. Bart's" had once been a large parish with an imposing church, school, and lyceum. By1980, most of the original congregation had moved from the neighborhood, and Joe's parish was a mix of former residents who maintained their affiliation; an older population of whites who remained in the neighborhood; African Americans, now the principal residents of the parish; and a scattering of people from different parts of the metropolitan area who chose to worship with Joe. Joe's impact on the parish was there to be seen if you looked or knew what to look for. He was, as usual, swimming upstream; assigned to a moribund inner city parish, but never for a moment letting his parishioners think he had any goal other than to turn it around into a small but vital parish community. One could readily see in his parishioners the confidence that he was indeed doing that. Their affection for him and its reciprocation were obvious. And there were the few "groupies"; those worshippers who were there because he was but lived in other communities. My family was among them, thus allowing me the opportunity to see the energy and hope his pastorate seemed to lend to that shrinking community. Indeed, it seemed that the out-migration stopped or slowed to a trickle during his tenure. But the most compelling testimony to the sentiments of his parishioners appeared a few months after his death in the dedication to the booklet prepared for the parish's Jubilee celebration. Those words say a great deal not only about his tenure there, but also about his influence generally on his congregations. Moreover, they were, despite his death, not words of resignation to gradual decline, but expression of a parish renaissance for which Joe's influence was clearly credited.

> In dedicating this Jubilee Booklet to Father Bissonette, we recall an extraordinary life brought to a tragic close during his seventh year as pastor of St. Bartholomew's. The contrasting emotions of this recollection mirror the paradox of a man committed to peace meeting a violent death at the hands of those he sought to help. Had Father Bissonette been an ordinary man we would expect his life and work to be magnified by the dramatic circumstances of his death. Sadly and happily, this is not the case. His work and accomplishments defy exaggeration now just as they overpowered his personal modesty while he lived.
>
> Father Bissonette's tenure as our pastor was a truly Pentecostal period in our history. He gave us

> strength, vision, and resolve when we were faced with daunting challenges to the very survival of our parish. By persistent hard work and the irresistible force of his personal example, he reestablished in our diminished and scattered numbers the vitality of a true human and spiritual community. His vision penetrated differences and helped us to weave the diverse strands of individuals and families into a fabric of community strengthened by its ties and enriched by its diversity. The impact of his life among us was vastly disproportionate to its few short years in our 75-year history. He gave us leadership, love, and finally, his life. But as we move with new vigor his memory and spirit will always live among us.

Later in 1980, Joe was elected president of the board of the Center for Justice, a role that positioned him for leadership in the various initiatives of the Center. A natural consequence was a powerful collegiality with the members, many of whom were there representing the religious communities which had initially formed the organization.

On March 24, 1980, Archbishop Oscar Romero was murdered in San Salvador because of his advocacy for the poor and, in the views of many in the peace and justice community, as a direct result of his opposition to the American-supported leadership in El Salvador. Later that year was the infamous murder of the four churchwomen by the military. Joe, at the time, was one of the activists sufficiently outraged to feel the need for some local response. The response took the form of the Medical Aid to El

Salvador Committee, an interdenominational group composed initially of members of the Center for Justice and the Western New York Peace Center, then under the leadership of Jim Mang. The Committee decided to launch an annual memorial Mass and public demonstration for Romero in order to keep attention on the political and social conditions in El Salvador and elsewhere in Central America where American policy was enabling if not causing widespread suffering for the poor and those advocating democratic government. From then until his death, Joe played a major role in the Romero commemoration as a frequent celebrant of the Mass, participant in and organizer of the public rally beforehand, and homilist.

Audrey Mang, Jim's wife and one of the principal leaders of the Western New York Peace Center, recalls a poignant remark in one of Joe's early homilies when he stated that, were his comments to be made in El Salvador, he would be marked for death. She asked him later for a copy of the homily but there was none. As was his pattern, he prepared intensely for his public remarks but delivered them without notes. Hetty Pasco, an Afro-American activist who continues to work for the poor on Buffalo's east side, remembered Joe's advocacy for the Central American poor in an article she wrote in 1996 for a weekly Buffalo newspaper, *The Criterion*: "He dedicated his life in service to the poor, voiceless, and powerless here in Western New York and the Central American countries where people are persecuted and swept aside by the powerful and greedy. I remember his saying, 'Those are my brothers and sisters they are starving and killing in Nicaragua and El Salvador.' "

Another of Audrey Mang's recollections stems from a program begun in conjunction with the Romero Mass and the Medical Aid to El Salvador Committee. The Committee joined with the local Los Ninos supporters for an annual El Salvador walk, which, like the dinner, was intended both to raise attention and funds. It was around 1983, before Audrey knew Joe well, and they fell into step for a time during the walk. At the time she was highly distressed over her daughter's child, who was being denied baptism for having been conceived out of wedlock. At the time, the prevailing and widely accepted traditional Church teaching was that the unbaptized were barred from entering heaven. For some reason, Audrey felt comfortable raising this concern with Joe during the walk. She recalls her immense sense of relief at his dismissal of this teaching as ridiculous. As he pointed out, followed to its logical conclusions, this doctrine would condemn every human being before Christ's life, as well as everyone living then or in the future who had never heard of Christ or chose not to believe in Him, to an afterlife significantly different from the relative minority of properly baptized Roman Catholics. What Audrey drew from this encounter, and remains convinced of today, is that she had encountered not simply a sympathetic priest but a true visionary. While there is nothing especially visionary about such a view among many Catholics today, this was 1983 when relatively few strongly devout Catholics truly questioned the official teachings from Rome, although their adherence, certainly in this country, was clearly slipping.

Joe's loss of innocence politically did not spill over into his basic personality, which, from my earliest memories, was characterized by a concern for others and humility bordering on self-effacement. To link that trait to something inherited from our mother is irresistible. She lived her life convinced that everyone else on earth had more important things to do than she. Among the curious aspects of a woman who would walk though fire for you was the fact that, in all our years in Buffalo, Gramma never once invited Ann and me to dinner, yet we and our kids still spent most Sunday evenings, often with Joe, having dinner at her apartment. But we always had to invite ourselves using some stratagem to put her at ease. Typically, Ann or I would call and say we had too much of something and could we bring it down and share it with her. That always worked and we would arrive to find the table set and a few little "things" from her freezer in process on the stove.

In light of that, Joe's reputation for never inviting anyone for dinner or any social occasion is almost eerie in its similarity. I remember the nuns at the Newman Center commenting with some irritation and disbelief about how Joe spent nearly every Tuesday evening there for dinner but never invited anyone to his place. Then, 14 years after Joe's death, I heard Weimer recall that behavior and attribute it to its real cause. As we were leaving a May 2001 meeting of the Bissonette Memorial Foundation trustees, Jack reminded me of how Joe would never extend a social invitation because he was sure he'd be *imposing* on someone. That Joe was not a Gandhi or Martin Luther King, Jr. may be attributed to many factors, but his diffidence virtually guaranteed it: he was incapable of self-promotion to the point where even taking appropriate credit for his accomplishments seemed either distasteful or discomfiting.

But that choice for the backseat was far more powerful than one might intuit. This power was expressed well by Esther Rae, an effective and respected activist who was Board Chairperson of the Buffalo affiliate of Women's Action for Nuclear Disarmament (WAND) at the time of Joe's death. Esther expressed a view echoed by others who worked with Joe. For them, his reluctance to jump to the front of the line was empowering to their own sense of their work. In a letter to our mother and the family after Joe's death she puts it well:

> Joe was a constant presence. His leadership was not the kind that required him to be at the top of the list, but he could always be found among the members and supporters of the various groups ... Joe was 'always there.' And what is most surprising to me now is the realization of what power and witness there is in that ministry. Work in social justice and peace is often looked upon with suspicion and carries moments of insecurity and doubt; it is during those moments that Joe's 'just being there' brought to mind once again the power of the Gospel, the presence of the Church, and affirmation and support of our work ... I think of him as a constant presence — of the Gospel and the Church community ... we struggle to believe that he continues for all of us to be 'always there.'

Surely predictive of this style was his "ambition" in life as expressed to Jack Weimer just after their ordination in 1958. Flush with the success of finally being ordained, they were discussing their futures. Weimer, doubtless considering the marks he and Joe would make on the world, turned to Joe and asked what his aspirations were. The reply was pure Joe: "I just want to be a good priest." Other characterizations reflect a similar theme: Bill Stanton, some years senior to Joe, always seemed intrigued by Joe's combination of integrity, courage, and gentleness and often called him "the gentle giant." Usually the reference would bring to Bill's mind a snapshot he once took of Joe reaching down to feed a semi-tame fawn. Yet it was the same Bill Stanton who described the same Joe as "the most confrontational priest in the diocese."

Sister Eileen O'Connor adds her recollections to the picture of Joe's ubiquitous quality. She recalls his work in preparations for the annual Romero Mass — coordinating with the other planners, deciding about the liturgy, and practicing the songs. And she underscores how he *always* showed up on the steps of City Hall, sometimes with only three or four others, to call public attention to the Latin American political situation. As her recollection ends, she strings together adjectives to describe him: simplicity, humility, lack of self-importance, openness, and sensitivity. From the tone and context of her remembrance it's clear she is contrasting Joe with at least some other priests in her experience. Again and again this search uncovers a seemingly paradoxical figure — humble, soft-spoken, ill-at-ease with praise or attention, friendly and humorous, but indomitable in facing down those who caused or profited from abuse of the weak and helpless.

Eileen's sentiments closely parallel those of Evelyn Brady, formerly a nun and now an educator in the Buffalo Schools. Another of Joe's great admirers, she published a recollection of Joe in *The Buffalo News* on the tenth anniversary of his death. In it she remembered his work but especially his commitment to non-violence and special sensitivity to women. She recalled his struggle with his own capacity for violence after standing in his rectory with a fireplace poker as an intruder attempted a break-in one night. But she concluded her column by noting what struck her so much about him: his habit of arriving early at meetings to make coffee, clearing the table, washing the dishes — tasks that, as she put it, "... seemed simple compared to Joe's serious and weighty concerns, yet in these ordinary chores, I came to know an extraordinary person [who] put the same kind of caring in setting a table as he put into his inspiring homilies." In concluding her recollection she states simply but compellingly:

> For the coming tenth anniversary of his death, there will be many memories of this giant of justice. I will be thinking of his extraordinary non-judgmental acceptance of everyone he met. I will remember how his brilliant intellect was deceptively hidden by his gentle presence. I will be reminded that his courage was never self-serving and that his commitment to justice was born of study, prayer, and compassion. And yes, I will remember how Joe stayed on till the last dish was put away. (*The Buffalo News*, February 15, 1997)

What Evelyn did not know was the sequel to the poker story. Joe had subsequently struggled with that incident because he knew his intention was to use it and he could never know what might have happened had the police not arrived before the intruder climbed in the window. The fact of his having planned the action troubled him because of its clash with his personal commitment to non-violence.

But the apprehension and jailing of the intruder presents an aspect of his values that may be lost in the totality of all-forgiving images. Whether Joe would have used the poker we'll never know, but he was angry and had no sympathy for the man despite numerous phone calls urging him not to press charges. Joe knew he was not a first time offender and was not about to pat him on the head. His reply to the man's last phone call from the holding center was, "You're where you belong and you should stay there." He was forgiving, accepting, and, to some, a sucker, but he had his limits.

Joan Malone worked closely with Joe in the years before his death. She was a Sister of St. Francis working at the Center for Justice when they met. Like others who knew him in those years, she recalls the many thankless and seemingly futile protests where Joe was always present to give encouragement and leadership. She speaks of his presence every Friday afternoon during Lent on the steps of City Hall to protest the Vietnam War; she remembers the protest of contra funding when a snowstorm reduced the turnout to a handful of people but Joe delivered his remarks nonetheless; she remembers the walkathons for Salvadoran refugees when she and Joe finished last and her suspicion that he slowed his pace for her; she remembers his leadership among those who in 1986 founded the Coalition for Economic Justice to stem the loss of jobs as Trico joined the maquiladoras movement on the Mexican-American border; and she remembers the Medical Aid to El Salvador dinners when Joe was in the kitchen. And through it all, like so many others, she remembers a priest who was different; a priest who was at the front of the line in the face of opposition or worse, indifference; yet, on the few occasions when the cameras were rolling, was rarely to be seen; a priest who was always there when discouragement and derision threatened to break the fragile ranks of those who took up the cause of the weak and voiceless. But, like Joe, she put herself on the line and reaped the discouragement from doing so. Largely due to that, his commitment and courage had special meaning for her, a meaning prompting her at least twice to express her thoughts to Joe in writing. In 1983 and again, in 1987, after his death, she put her thoughts on paper. Her 1983 letter to Joe captures many of the sentiments I heard expressed in interviews and in less formal conversation with religious and others who were his colleagues during those years he fought for justice but found no support and even opposition in his own Church.

Her words:

> I want to tell you how much it means to me that you are the person you are ... committed to a more just world. I have some sense of how much of yourself you give, how much you put on the line

> ... I can only have a sense. I understand that the hard moments come for each of us and only each of us knows their toll ... I get so discouraged ... but then I remember you ... and my disillusionment with the Church just isn't so significant anymore ... the committed person you are, who knows the risks and acts, is the gospel I believe in ... I want to thank you for all that, for this gift you have been giving me.

Joe responded a few days later acknowledging their common feeling of being on the "fringe" of the Church, in a city with a "very cautious leadership." Typically, he refrains from accusatory comments despite the pariah status he must have felt from the hierarchy. His note also confirms my conviction of the powerful mutual support that sustained those who were indeed on the fringe. He closes by saying, "Your letter certainly made my day and days." But his carefully worded note about "cautious leadership" was some distance from his true feelings about a leadership he then considered and described elsewhere as simply "dead."

Joan Malone was another of Joe's friends and colleagues whose relationship with him spun off another prong of activism in the community. In 1986, when it was clear that Trico intended to move out of Buffalo, a local union leader, Norm Harper, turned to Joe for help. Joe's involvement was quickly followed by other concerned clergy and laypersons. Among the clergy were Robert Beck and Robert Grimm, both highly respected leaders in the Protestant ministry whose vision extended well beyond denominational lines. (Grimm at the time was Executive Director of the area Council of Churches). That ad hoc group managed to delay the relocation, a slim victory for the Trico workers, but their efforts resulted in the formation of the Coalition for Economic Justice that continues as the key regional not for profit organization advocating for employee rights. Joan Malone became its first professional director. In September 2004, Bob Grimm remembered the leadership of that initial group in his remarks accepting the Coalition's Robert P. Beck award.

The recollections of the nuns and others were largely of the period during which Joe's true vocation was reaching clarity and fulfillment. His simple post-ordination aspiration to be "a good priest" was becoming defined for him and those around him. That period was recapped well in Jack Weimer's homily at the funeral Mass. Worth repeating in full, it tells of Joe's work and its meaning to those who knew it.

"Absorb the violence
don't reflect it
Absorb the violence"

> Dan Berrigan's words. Joe used them in a talk he gave for Daybreak Productions — a talk on peace and justice. I used them Sunday in my homily. Joe lived them somewhere between 9:30 and 11:30 Tuesday night.
>
> It was the culmination of a life lived after the pattern of Christ. We gather today confident in hope that as he has died in Christ so will he share in Christ's resurrection. For this we sing, alleluia

— but we do it with tears in our hearts.

The last two days we heard it from our brother priests — that Joe was for us a conscience — a living challenge to our integrity and our education. Not that he ever judged us or put us down. His life was his message — and his message was the gospel of peace — the gospel of justice. He chose the central city because he saw Christ's concern for the marginalized, the disenfranchised. From that base his ministry spread from the Delevan-Grider Neighborhood Organization, the action for Trico workers to chairing the Board of the Center for Justice to chairing the Medical Aid to El Salvador Committee to chairing the Annual Mass in memory of Archbishop Romero, to demonstrating against the administration's policy in Nicaragua, hosting refugees stranded along the American-Canadian border.

And all this in the past few months.

Joe lived what has become the official policy of the Catholic Church — a preferential option for the poor. He had disengaged himself from the American passion for things. He had an easy disregard for material goods. His car would be dignified by calling it a wreck. He lived simply and generously. For ten years he refused an offer of a free place to stay in Florida for a week in January because he felt it was not seemly for him to enjoy such a luxury when his people could not. He never said that we should not go, just that he could not go.

Prophet? I guess it fits, but that wasn't it. Joe had too fine a mind to be an ideologue. He knew that good people could disagree on ends and means. But that did not immobilize him. When the moment came, Joe spoke his word, performed his act. And he did it with a consistency, a commitment to principle that often infuriated people in authority and made the rest of us uneasy in our chairs of prudent counsel.

What more needs to be said? I fear Joe might chide me that this has been too much of a eulogy — not enough a homily. He knew the difference.

Perhaps the charge sticks — but I think not. When the man and the message are so much one, to speak the man is to proclaim the message.

In the end it comes down to this. Joe chose to be with and for those most oppressed. He once said that to be close to the poor you must expect to share their fate. He understood there were no safe places. He lived too close to where poverty and despair lash out in violence — and so they murdered him.

We mourn for Joe but we also mourn for our society that locks people in cycles of poverty, that impoverishes social programs to finance ever more deadly instruments of destruction, that disenfranchises the unborn, the emotionally disturbed, minority groups, and the elderly. We mourn a world wracked with war and hatred and personal violence. We cry over Jerusalem that fails to hear Christ's word of peace — of justice. We mourn our own lives that continue to be shaped by revenge, racism, and greed. We mourn — and our only hope is Christ who said, 'Blessed are they who mourn — they shall be comforted.'

So farewell good friend and Alleluia, we will miss you. And now who will be our conscience?

Enjoying a joke with nephew Brian, 1977.

CHAPTER SIXTEEN

NEARING THE END

Joe's support of the refugees, coupled with his growing opposition to U.S. policy in Central America, created an irony for my wife and me, an irony born of our ignorance of the real nature and extent of his work and mission. The consequences would appear shortly after Joe's death in an unfortunate clash with some of Joe's closest colleagues.

Bonny Butler, now an attorney with Neighborhood Legal Services, describes her relationship with Joe in the years before his death through the period when he was chairman of the Center for Justice. Her work with Joe was principally on the Medical Aid to El Salvador Committee. I knew nothing of her until just after his death when the only suspects in his murder were two refugees who had been living on the third floor of his rectory at the time. When we learned of their presence, Ann and I arranged through Jack Weimer to meet at his home with Bonny and Kathleen Rimar — an immigration attorney and leader in the early years of the asylum movement in Buffalo — to learn what we could about them. Joe was killed on a Tuesday and we met the following evening. We both felt at the time a desperate need to do whatever we could to learn about the circumstances of his death and perhaps assist in finding the killer(s).

In July of 1984, Bonny had become the first director of VIVE, the principal agency in Buffalo serving refugees from Latin America. Joe was among the key supporters of this work and, along with other priests in the area, was housing refugees in the years before an actual residence was established. Bonny's presence at the meeting was because of her knowledge of the refugees placed with Joe.

During the meeting, Ann was taking detailed notes and periodically interrupting the conversation for clarification. Bonny, I recall, was noticeably uncomfortable as her words were being recorded, but forthcoming nonetheless. As we spoke, it became clear that neither Bonny, Kathy, nor their colleagues in the refugee program had any suspicion whatever of the two men who had been at Joe's and were, at the time of the meeting, in police custody. Nor did Ann and I realize that as we were attempting to learn more about the refugees' possible involvement in the murder, Bonny, Kathy and others were working to get them released from custody.

A good part of Bonny's discomfort could have arisen from those competing agendas.

In our ignorance of Joe's closeness with those individuals, as well as his formal involvement with the sanctuary movement, Ann and I had steered into a collision course with an entire bloc of Joe's friends and kindred spirits. In fact, in our single mindedness that night about collecting information on the murder, we missed altogether the clues in front of us pointing to the imminent crash. Had our agenda been other than what it was, we might have learned more of Joe's life in the 1980s; a life enmeshed in the refugee movement in concert with a handful of local priests, nuns, and laypersons, actively supporting the work of VIVE and, in those early days, quietly housing Central American refugees much in the fashion of the Underground Railroad.

The collision would occur shortly after the meeting at Weimer's. Neither Ann nor I had any realization of the role of Bonny and her colleague, Kathy, in attempting to release the refugees from custody, but after our meeting they secured their release with the voluntary assistance of Mark Mahoney, a highly skilled criminal lawyer. The nun into whose custody they were released was Sister Karen Klimczak, then operating an early release program for convicts out of a former convent on Sycamore Street. She was already housing about twenty refugees on the third floor of the building where Joe's guests, Juan and Jose, were then lodged. But on the Friday following Joe's funeral, Dennis Vacco, the assistant district attorney handling the case, was granted a bench warrant from Judge Theodore Kasler to return them to custody as flight risks. Kasler set cash bail of $50,000 each. The nuns, and others convinced of their innocence, were devastated but far from defeated. First they prayed, interestingly, to Joe, and then went to the holding center to talk to the refugees before they were questioned by the police. Later on Friday and again on Saturday, they met at the Peace Center to discuss their situation and plan a strategy for releasing the refugees. The plan that emerged was a rally and prayer vigil to be held at the First Presbyterian Church on Sunday. The rally was to have three components: a public prayer petition, attraction of public attention to the refugees' plight, and securing bail money for their release. During the Friday meeting, the bail issue was essentially guaranteed by someone who pledged to post whatever funds were not raised at the rally.

About the time this was happening, Ann and I received a call from Vacco asking us to meet with him Saturday morning to review what information he then had. Under pressure to release the refugees and lacking sufficient grounds to charge them, he was reaching for any shred of evidence and hoped we might help him find it. We, however, were ignorant of his legal situation with the two refugees, knowing only that they were in custody and not learning until Saturday morning that Kasler was pressing Vacco to charge or release them. Present also at the meeting was the district attorney's office investigator, a former Buffalo police detective, John Montando, who spoke with conviction of the refugees' guilt. Because of our inexperience, this certitude, expressed by a seasoned investigator, lent credibility to the possibility that the refugees were guilty.

The meeting, which was supposed to be an hour or two, lasted all day. In the course of discussing a variety of suspicious circumstances, such as the fact that one of the refugees was carrying a large amount of cash and was not from the country he had originally claimed, we involved John LaFalce who contacted some officials in Central America but added little to Vacco's vacuous case. Still, there were questions unanswered when we left late in the day. One in particular that seized my interest was a suspected bloodstain on the wall of the staircase leading to the second and third floors. Vacco said it was being analyzed at a State Police lab but the results were not yet back. Ann and I considered that as major potential evidence but at the same time wondered why something of that import would not simplify the continued custody of the refugees. Interestingly, we never heard another thing about it one way or the other. Perhaps it had been a stratagem, wishful thinking, or became academic after the arrest and confession of the killers.

Ann and I returned home late Saturday afternoon, and the phone rang almost immediately. It was Bonny Butler telling us enthusiastically of the planned rally and vigil. My response was negative, fearing that an immediate release of the refugees would forever foreclose learning the answers to the questions pending from our meeting. We not only wouldn't attend, but were opposed to the whole idea. Bonny's voice changed instantly and she put Kathy

Rimar on the phone, probably in hopes that I would be more sympathetic once I understood the legal issues and the tenuous validity of Vacco's effort to hold the refugees. I was not, however, impressed by this, believing that a couple more days of custody would be a small price in the event the refugees were the perpetrators or otherwise involved. In my thinking at the time, their status as refugees would vastly limit the possibility of their being found again should any of the unanswered questions, e.g., the blood stain, point to their involvement. Although I saw Kathy Rimar once or twice since that conversation, it was the last time we spoke. Within days of Joe's death, my wife and I had alienated a large number of Joe's closest friends and colleagues. Only recently have I learned of the extent of that network; at the time I thought it limited to a few people involved in countering Vacco's legal maneuvering.

As it later turned out, during the murder, the refugees were on the third floor watching television and because of that, the size of the house, and Joe's failure to call up to them, they never knew about the murder until the police arrived.

Sunday morning we received another phone call. This one was from Dennis Vacco who asked if I knew someone named Teddy Simmons. The night before, Joe's real killers, Theodore Simmons and Milton Jones, had "done" another priest.

The victim this time was Monsignor David Herlihy, who, in his retirement, was living at another east side rectory, St. Matthew's.

His murder was even more grisly than Joe's. He died as Joe did. Incredibly the night might have been worse. Before going to the rectory at St. Matthew's, Jones and Simmons appeared at the convent of the parish. The nun who answered the door saw two black youths on the porch. One, Teddy Simmons, was at the door and another, larger boy, Milton Jones, stood back in the shadows. Simmons asked to use the phone. With a presence of mind that surely saved her life and probably others, she kept the storm door hooked and offered to make the call for them. Teddy Simmons gave her a number. She left to call, only to find it a non-working number. When she returned to the door the boys were gone. Soon after, they were at the rectory door, but this time prepared to gain entry without recourse to ruse.

Monsignor Herlihy's body was found on March 8, approximately 12:50 a.m. Earlier that evening, Teddy Simmons had arrived at Milton Jones's house on Ivy Street where the two sat and listened to music. The grocery money from St. Bartholomew's had apparently run out. Teddy said he was broke but knew where they could get some money by "doing" another priest. They walked to St. Matthew's. After the unsuccessful stop at the convent, they went to the rectory. There they were met by Monsignor Herlihy who was alone in the house because the pastor was out on an errand. Teddy forced his way in the front door then let Milton in a side entrance. After emptying the safe, they tied Monsignor Herlihy in a chair with duct tape (they had come prepared this time), broke a lamp fixture over his head, and stabbed him to death. The boys then ran, and Milton went to the home of his friend, William, on Fougeron Street. The two played video games for several hours then went to an all night convenience store about 2:00 a.m. where they met Teddy. Teddy and Milton decided they wanted to get some girls and would go to Toronto. They hailed a cab and paid the driver $135 in advance for the trip. At Canadian customs on the Peace Bridge, they were sent back for lack of identification. While returning through the American side they encountered a suspicious customs officer who ran a computer check and found an outstanding bench warrant on Jones, who was detained. The police were called, and they returned Jones to the New York State Division for Youth detention center where he was supposed to be in custody. Teddy, meanwhile, caught a plane for San Diego where he had a brother. After delivering Milton, the police learned of the second murder and began an investigation that by the next day tied both boys to the crime. They returned to the detention center in the morning and asked for Milton. As he came down the stairs they asked him, "You know why we're here Milton?" He nodded and quietly said "yes."

The next day, Teddy was arrested in San Diego and brought back. Both confessed during interrogation. No lawyers were involved until they had assigned counsel at arraignment. Had they been represented initially, they might never have been convicted or at least been able to plead to a lesser charge. Their signed confessions combined with Teddy's talk in the plane about shielding the priests from Milton offered the prosecution and jury a running start on the guilty verdict. Both were sentenced to consecutive terms of twenty-five years. In 2004, Milton turned 35 and Teddy 36; each had 33 years remaining to serve. Their survival, at least in Milton's case is doubtful. Milton, perhaps because of his size, willingness to fight back, and rejection of sexual liaisons, has been beaten repeatedly by guards and prisoners and, while both he and Teddy have been on suicide watch, Milton has made at least one attempt. His letters and immersion in Muslim and Christian scripture are an extended but futile cry for help. Serious depression underscored by a suicide attempt led to his removal from Attica to a mental health treatment facility, an unusual move indicative of serious mental disorder. Teddy has been moved often, probably for his safety, and most recently was reassigned to a facility downstate. I was to have seen both of them at Attica in March of 2004, but both had been relocated some weeks earlier. Milton was released from the treatment facility and transferred to Wende Correctional Facility outside Buffalo where Sister Karen Klimszak and I saw him on May 17, 2004. It was my fourth visit to Joe's killers.

Standing during sentencing for the murders. At left is defendent Milton Jones; Theodore Simmons is on the right. Photo by Richard W. Roeller. Taken on November 1, 1988; *Buffalo News* file photo.

CHAPTER SEVENTEEN

TEDDY, MILTON, AND JOE

When my son, Brian, was in middle school, he simply had to have a particular kind of bike that was all the rage at the time, a Spider. I remember thinking it was a pretty impractical bike of limited utility, but I was overruled and bought the bike. As I had suspected, it was not long in reaching obsolescence for Brian and most of his contemporaries. So we put an ad in the paper to sell it and one Sunday afternoon, while I was in the basement, the phone rang. A young boy with an unmistakable Afro-American accent was calling to respond. Among the questions he asked was "Where do you *stay* at?" I was and continue to be struck by that expression for home. To me it conveyed a lamentable sense of rootlessness, especially for a child. The next time I thought about that was during the trials of Teddy Simmons and Milton Jones. They had nearly reached adulthood, (Teddy was 18 and Milton 17 at the time of the murders) in circumstances of similar absence of permanency and belonging. While this may be the norm and neither peculiar nor problematic in a culture of multi-generational families, for me it represented a gross lack of what I and others considered fundamental nurturance. My judgment on this is largely subjective, but somewhere in their development, something did or did not happen that enabled them to behave in a way that continues to escape my comprehension.

Joe had told Ann Hastee about Simmons, who had periodically appeared at the church looking for handouts and offering numerous excuses for needing help. Joe was very uncomfortable having him around and told Ann that he thought Simmons was unstable. Joe clearly never suspected that Simmons's familiarity with the rectory and church would evolve into a plan to rob and murder. Perhaps Joe's instincts were picking up signals of something far more than instability. Whenever the plan was conceived, Simmons knew he needed help. At some time in the winter of 1987, Milton Jones was recruited. Jones may have been an opportunistic accomplice, or, as most involved believed, chosen for his size and known capacity for physical violence — a capacity paradoxically combined with a reputation among acquaintances and teachers for gentleness.

Milton, at the age of 17, was 6'4" tall and weighed well over 200 pounds. He was already the father of an infant and had been sentenced earlier in the year to a New York State youth detention center for a bike theft incident in which he had injured another youth with a pipe or similar piece of metal. Despite that incident, however, he was not, at least in the view of teachers, coaches and other adults who knew him, considered a violent or dangerous young man. What his reputation on the street was, I don't know. But Teddy managed to recruit him to assist in an easy job of robbing a rectory where he knew the priest in residence. Whether he knew Joe's housemate, Bob Stolinski, or even of him is not clear, but I suspect for Jones and Simmons he was either unknown or discounted.

Stolinski was full time chaplain at Erie County Medical Center on Grider Street opposite the rectory. Because he was seldom around in the daytime, it is quite likely that Teddy had not encountered him during his previous visits to the rectory. My recollection of the events of February 24, and subsequent conversations and news reports, does not connect Stolinski with Simmons in any way before the murder. Joe's relationship with Stolinski was fairly limited; from time to time they would have dinner together either at the rectory, or, more likely, out at a restaurant. Beyond that, they pretty much simply shared the rectory with minimal personal connection. This was easy enough, given the fact that the rectory was built In the 1930s when congregations were large and living accommodations provided for as many as five priests in residence. It was Stolinski who discovered the crime scene when he returned home the evening of February 24, 1987. He was shaken badly by the discovery and, to my knowledge, never resumed residence there. As the one who discovered Joe's body, he was required to testify at the trials. From the time of the murder until the beginning of the first trial, over a year had passed during which time I had not seen him other than briefly at the funeral home where I recall hearing him conducting a prayer service for a group of people assembled near the casket. The next time I saw him was the night before the trial when he was being prepared by assistant district attorney Vacco for his testimony the next day. I shook his hand, which was limp, cold, and saturated with sweat. I remember thinking him a pathetic figure, a reaction surely due in large measure to my general annoyance about the number of priests whom I considered to have chosen celibacy for the wrong reasons.

My annoyance stemmed mainly from a longstanding and strong admiration for Joe's choice of celibacy. To me it was always immense in its negation of everything I and most people considered not only important but essential — money, family, status, and "things." Joe not only rejected all of that, he refused to devalue those whose sacrifice was less or, for whom it was no sacrifice at all but a career by default. If my feelings were shared by Joe, neither I nor anyone would ever know it. This was one more aspect of his combination of acceptance of others coupled with a habit of dismissing anything special about himself or his actions. To me, Stolinski and some other priests I had met were the antithesis of Joe and most other priests I knew; in my eyes, they diminished the sacrifice of celibacy.

One of the defenses offered at the trial by Milton's court-appointed attorney team was that he was coerced by Simmons into participating in the robberies and murders. On its face this was unconvincing, a point driven home by Vacco's comparison of the physical size of the two defendants. In fact, Vacco capped off this contrast when he asked one of the witnesses if Simmons was known on the street as a nerd. The immediate objection of the defense attorneys was sustained, but the point was made.

Until the trial, I had seen neither Milton nor Teddy in person. My first sight of Milton was a bit shocking but also confirmatory. The first day of the first trial, as Milton was being led from the courtroom and passed in front of us, he glanced slowly toward his family, mother and stepfather, nodding almost imperceptibly with a steadiness intended to convey control and "cool." I had been, and continue to be, incapable of grasping the capacity for savagery of both young men, but as I saw that look — to me the reptilian, vacant eyes of a predator — I "knew" that the gratuitous cruelty was possible. But the "how" was then and now a mystery. Who or what transforms a human infant into a reptile in the space of a few years? Later I learned that my initial impression was probably wrong on at least two counts: Milton turned out to be far more complex than that, and the blank, unfeeling stare with lids at "half mast" was the standard look of the streets where these boys grew up. The deliberate, unhurried steps of the large animal, however, I was to see again when he entered the visitors' hall at Attica State Correctional Facility during the first visit by Ann and me.

Our visits to the two boys were specifically and exclusively to learn, if possible, what could have explained the savagery of the killings. Ordinarily, such brutal abandon betrays an uncontrolled outburst of passion, which in turn suggests a relationship of some depth and duration. Joe's knowledge of Simmons was no more than that mentioned earlier and Jones's appearance at his door on February 24 was the first meeting for both. Milton was an enigma from that standpoint alone and grew more so to me as I came to know him. It became easy to understand the shock of family, teachers, and coaches at Milton's involvement in two such horrifying attacks. Joe was bludgeoned then stabbed ten times with a hunting knife. Monsignor Herlihy suffered an even more vicious attack. Milton seemed an unlikely monster. On initial impression he was soft spoken, controlled, and seemingly gentle — a gentle giant (ironically, the very term frequently applied to Joe by his friend Bill Stanton).

Milton entered the visitors' hall and scanned the area curiously. Still puzzled, he moved through the tables with a loping stride unchanged from when we had last seen him in the courtroom five years earlier. Unbeknownst to us, he had not been told whom to expect, nor had he been visited by anyone at all in months if not years. It was February 4, 1992, nearly five years since the murder.

Several weeks before, I had decided to move on a promise made to myself years earlier — to learn more about how Joe died and why. When I mentioned my plans to my wife, Ann, she decided immediately to go with me. I had expected her to be at least ambivalent about my going but she was eager to join me, albeit equally apprehensive. Since our move to Buffalo in 1970, she had come to regard Joe as her own brother and her affection for him was easily equal to my own.

The vague discomfort that began with the decision to make the visit began to find definition on entering the prison. The staff at the reception desk asked for his cell number and block, neither of which we knew so we were presented with a form which, among other things, required us to specify our relationship to the prisoner. Reluctantly and haltingly, we entered "friend." The computer was, of course, "down" and we were shunted to a small waiting area where we sat for at least an hour furtively watching the other visitors, trying to imagine their circumstances and relationships to the inmates. All were females; most appeared to be girlfriends or wives and several were accompanied by children. Directly across from us were two women appearing to be in their forties. Based on their audible discussion of scripture, we concluded that they, like us, were there on business. The others were not on business, and, unlike us, clearly knew the system.

The prominent sign on the wall, obviously newly installed, triggered all kinds of fantasies about its recent need in a prison already there for decades. Printed in Spanish and English, the sign proscribed tube tops, deep necklines, open backs, or shorts with inseams less than six inches. I wondered if the new rules had resulted from the current publicity about former Washington, D.C., Mayor, Marion Barry, who had allegedly had sex with a female visitor during a visit.

Once our names were called, we presented ourselves for physical clearance. Here, we placed shoes, any metal objects, and all pocket contents in a tray then passed through a metal detector. (The intrusive observation that, as this is written ten years later during a period of the most intensive airport security in history, a man nearly blew up a passenger jet with explosives concealed in his shoes, is irresistible.) We crossed a courtyard and entered the main building where we were again halted for identification and checked against a list of visitors approved for Milton Jones. As first-time visitors we were not on the list so another form was completed that he would have to approve to permit subsequent visits. Having cleared this checkpoint we stood before a massive iron gate operated by a guard behind one-way glass. From there, we followed a corridor leading to a room resembling a German *bierhalle* — spacious and barren with row after row of small tables. The attending guard here reviewed our papers and issued curt directions, "Row four, number six." Seeing no numbers, we were confused. My vacant look at the guard was met with an impatient repetition of the same instructions. I was already angry and we were only visiting. We had been offered a miniscule glimpse of life without freedom. With Ann's help we found our table and waited another forty-five minutes. By now we had been at the facility over two hours, believing that Milton had been notified well in advance of our arrival. Given that assumption, we began to think he had chosen not to see us. When he did come into view we again assumed he knew who was there. We were wrong on both counts. He arrived in the room knowing only that he had a visitor at row four, number six, where we saw each other for the first time since his trial began five years earlier in 1988.

He approached us slowly and tentatively. When he stood at our table, I asked if he knew us. He said he knew I was Ray but didn't know Ann. I invited him to sit down and told him why we were there. It was already clear this would be nothing like any of us had envisioned. My notebook with my list of questions remained under my chair, not resting on the expected Formica table. Nor was there any phone with which to talk through a Plexiglas window. The cabaret sized tables, with me knee-to-knee with one of Joe's killers was not in my anticipated script, nor was note-taking in this one. His discomfort and the tension among the three of us were palpable. But the tension had not begun just then. Slowly and with low voltage it had started some weeks earlier when I decided the fifth anniversary would be the time to look for the answers only two people knew. Milton was first.

From the beginning, the apparently gratuitous savagery was as mystifying as it was horrifying. And, I wanted to know what those final minutes were like for Joe, although my ambivalence about knowing the truth was powerful. But the overarching question was a bigger one: how could two young men, one legally unable to vote, drink, or drive after dark, stalk then repeatedly bludgeon and stab another human being? The brutality was all out of proportion to any evident motivating factors: no explosive anger, no revenge, not even resistance. Indeed, minutes earlier Joe had been preparing sandwiches for them — a meal — the quintessential primal bond transcending barriers of language, culture, and age. True, he had a superficial prior acquaintance with Simmons and could identify them as the robbers, so perhaps he had to die. But that did not and does not explain the blood lust evident in both murders. How can two boys in their late teens be capable of this? Was there some displaced rage that crowded out any natural inhibitions to kill?

Perhaps there were no inhibitions to begin with. I have often wondered if these two approached adulthood without internalizing even rudimentary sensitivities or if these sensitivities had been already extinguished over the short span of 17 years. Something incomprehensible to me allowed for an intimate, close-up, and relatively prolonged butchery of another human being followed days later by the same thing. Certainly, examples of similar attacks abound, but usually there is anger, intoxication, a situation spinning out of control, or some combination. Yes, inexperienced killers would be unaware that killing with a four-inch blade hunting knife would not be easy or fast (a fact that Terry Anderson would point out to me years later during an appearance for the Bissonette Foundation), but their repetition of the act ten days later indicates no second thoughts after Joe's murder; if anything, they were emboldened, judging from their subsequent admission that after Joe's successful robbery and murder they decided to "*do* another priest." My incredulity drove me to Attica and later to Auburn State Prison.

After four years of avoidance, the big step of clearing a date and arranging the visit had taken only a few minutes. Then the low volume nagging was replaced by apprehension, not fear of the encounter, but the reluctance to see it all straight on. I didn't know what I'd learn, but it would be more than I knew then and the small comfort many of us clung to about Joe having been knocked unconscious before the knifing began might be lost. Frequently, while awaiting the trip to Attica, I was reminded of the time I had nicked the ends of my fingers with a chain saw and kept my fist clenched fearing to look at what might have happened. It was the same kind of "head-in-the sand" behavior. Now the sand was cleared and we began.

I explained to Milton why we had come, emphasizing that this was not a peace offering. He started to speak barely audibly, beginning with how the plan by him and Teddy had evolved. Simmons had told Milton several days beforehand (prior to February 24, 1987) that he knew where they could "get some money." Milton didn't need money, but neither did he make decisions for himself in those days. According to plan, they arrived together at the front door of St. Bartholomew's rectory at 9:30 p.m. Joe had just finished two meetings with parish groups and was preparing to leave for a party at a nearby parish. He went to the door and found the boys there complaining that they were hungry and had no place to go. Joe invited them in and asked them to sit in a side room off the front hall while he went to the kitchen. From that, one would think he intended not to bring them into the house and perhaps bring them something and send them on their way. However, later the police discovered two places set at the kitchen table and the makings for baloney sandwiches, none of which had been touched. While he was preparing the food, the boys walked through the hallway and came up behind him with a hunting knife carried by Teddy. When Joe turned to face them, Teddy asked if he believed in God. Joe's response, with a quizzical expression on his face, was affirmative, to which Teddy replied, "That's good because you're going to meet Him." Joe tried unsuccessfully to convince Teddy to put the knife down.

As Milton related these facts we strained to hear because, in his struggling efforts to remain composed, he spoke in a near whisper. As he described Joe's words to Teddy he stopped and asked if we could do this later. Thinking he meant at another visit, we began to get up, but he stopped us, asking haltingly if we would not go but just wait. He wondered if we could talk about something else for a while. Since I knew something about his life from the trials and the extensive media coverage, I asked him about his family and what he had been doing since his arrest. He had spent over a year In the Erie County Holding Center until the trials were completed. From there he was sent to a facility called Comstock for another year, then transferred to Attica where he had been for nearly three years when we arrived.

Although only 20 when entering Attica, he learned quickly that life "inside" was dangerous and cruel, especially for a convicted priest killer. He had the unhappy fortune to be hated by all the guards and most of the prisoners as well. For him, there was no place to hide. Traditional beliefs about honor codes among thieves and prisoners are romantic myths to begin with, but some crimes carry a special stigma, especially to staff that will quickly single out perpetrators of those offenses. Milton was marked immediately for the standard treatment — provocation by guards who would then find it necessary to "subdue" him. He described an early incident where he was braced against the bars, a standard method to conduct a body search. But his frisking included two crushing grips to his testicles intended to make him break position. Knowing what was planned, he remained in position to avoid the beating that would ensue otherwise. In passing that test he remained relatively unmolested for a while although careful to avoid occasions for violence. The abuse by guards and other inmates would resume and actually intensify in subsequent years.

Contrary to my expectations, life inside is quite unstructured and almost monastic. Prisoners don't all march in lockstep to daily jobs but are assigned to or sometimes select "programs." Milton's program was education. In February of 1992 he had completed 33 college level credits, a semester beyond completion of an associate's degree in social sciences. The education was a central feature of his life and he took great pride in his accomplishments. His conversation was a collage of contrasting languages, bouncing back and forth between sophisticated, aptly used terminology, such as "ideology," and street patois in describing his interrogation: " The police pounded on the table and had us all skeered up." He had learned to think in systems terms about himself and others in his circumstances. His explanatory model for the world is conflict in which individuals are in constant struggle against exploitation by society, the state, and bureaucrats, including, of course, those who run prisons. Quite astutely, I thought, he used the example of how the prison system needed him and other prisoners as much as society needed prisons. To his keepers he ascribed a calculus of maximizing gain that, however deliberate and accurate, is unlikely to be articulated or even thought of at a conscious level in many individuals. In response to my question about the source of his theories, he allowed that they derived from his experience, studies, and personal reading. To manage the cynicism of such a harsh worldview he had converted to Islam, finding trustworthy people only among those devoted to God and Allah.

Perhaps as exculpatory rationalization, the oppression motif is applied as well to his own childhood and teen years. It rises to meet the question, the big question for us, what accounts for the capacity for deadly violence, and, for a time at least, lack of remorse. A disjointed depiction of oppression, lack of adult male guidance, and victimization — rape at the age of five, racially motivated assault, and ridicule by peers — unfolds. Always, however, he adds quickly a disclaimer of any attempt to justify or excuse the murder or diminish its gravity. Nothing, he insists, can "compensate" us for what he did. And still there is a portrayal of passivity and bad judgment, a bid for some absolution, or at least acceptance by us of something other than the pure malevolence widely attributed to him and Teddy. Delivered in measured, gentle speech, eye contact steady and anxiety apparent, it's easy to believe. Then you remind yourself and him that he did it twice in ten days and between times was seen sharpening the hunting knife on an electric grinding wheel. Again he steps backstage and his response returns on an angle. That wheel didn't really sharpen it, it only roughed it up, and it didn't belong to him, but to an acquaintance, Robert Narocki. His awkward efforts to distance himself from the savagery of his behavior seemed intended partly to minimize our condemnation but at least as much to support his own struggle to square his behavior with his self-image.

That disconnect between what he was capable of and how he and others saw him is vividly reflected in two of our conversations while at Attica. On the first visit I asked him if anyone else came to visit. He said he had very few visitors or contact of any sort with anyone from the outside, including the woman who used to write. Inquiring about her, I learned of a chance encounter he had several months before Joe's murder at a bus stop on Elmwood Avenue after leaving school. He was about to board a crowded bus when he noticed an adult white woman behind him. Knowing she would not get on if he did, he stepped aside and let her board ahead of him. As he expected, she was the last one on and the door was closed leaving him on the street. She looked at him from the window as the bus pulled away and some time later met him again at the same stop. Then she thanked him and offered him a dollar. He refused the money and stated to me, in a quite matter of fact manner, that it was "no big deal, I know my manners." Hearing that statement in the context of what we were discussing was staggering. Here was a young man who had repeatedly stabbed two total strangers telling me he knew his manners. Then during the second visit an incident occurred lending more credence to the belief that we were talking to someone with incredible capacity for compartmentalizing feelings and behavior. Ann got up to go to the coffee machine and while she was gone he looked across the table and asked to see my hand. Puzzled, I extended my hand toward him and he took it firmly in both of his. Then he looked at me and said, "I'm sorry about your brother." There were tears in his eyes, real ones. Later, when I went for coffee the same thing happened with Ann. Ann's reaction was captured in an article by Donn Esmonde appearing in *The Buffalo News* on February 23, 1997, following our first visit. "That's what he told us — that nothing he could do would ever compensate for what he'd done — I never felt he was putting on an act." Esmonde's piece ended with a brief but prescient conclusion about what was set in motion by the decision to make that initial visit.

> Next week the Bissonettes will go back to Attica. Jones will be waiting. They have more questions. He says he'll have answers. For the Bissonettes it's another foray into uncharted territory, a search for resolution that may not exist. But there the three will be: the brother and sister-in-law of the victim, and one of the murderers, bound by circumstance into an odd covenant. Dependent on each other for that most elusive of ends, peace of mind.

Some amalgam of revisionist autobiography and serious retrospection defines him from childhood as the reactor. Having been "whupped" in fourth grade after a poor report card, he settled into school and came, in time, to see it as his principal job as a young man. For him, that was a matter of conscious choice carrying well beyond the insistence of his mother. But school was his only deliberate choice. In other areas he followed, imitated, and sought to please. His moral code was chameleon-like, taking on the color of whomever he was attached to at the time. As a physically precocious boy, that subservience would occasionally result in violence. Serious injury inflicted on another boy in a dispute over a bicycle led to his detention in a New York State Division for Youth facility the year before he killed Joe. Yet that violence was, in his view, a matter of following another's lead. He never saw himself as belligerent or dangerous nor, indeed, did others. Classmates at McKinley High regarded him as a "big Teddy Bear" and staff of the New York State Division for Youth saw no need to detain him as he came and went at will from their facility, even though under court order to be in physical custody. Students and faculty at McKinley expressed shock and disbelief after his arrest. He seemed serious, compliant, and harmless — qualities he projects still that lent a surreal character to our conversations.

Whatever a murderer is supposed to be like, Milton doesn't quite fit. The incontrovertible proof, plus his own admission of guilt, do little to dispel a sense of unreality. That this person is capable of willful violence let alone unprovoked gruesome savagery defies comprehension without some exotic and extravagant psychological interpretations. A mere pedestrian effort to make sense of it resolves into a picture of a youth so desperate for acceptance that he could be manipulated to any extent by anyone whose approval he valued. All this fits his personal presentation until you remember the image of him standing alone (no audience expected) in his room working the hunting knife on a grinder in preparation for "doing" priest number two. That image speaks to you what it spoke to the jury: a willful, cold-blooded killer. Still, the young man at the table doesn't fit that description for a moment. But somewhere in that placid persona was a violence incredible both in its fury and its capacity to recede as quickly and deeply as the speed and ferocity of its emergence.

Curiously, another gentle giant was his victim, but in this case, the characterization fit right off the rack. Joe was 6'3" tall and weighed around two hundred pounds. For his generation, that was large. He was healthy and a lifelong athlete, still playing squash twice a week with Jack Weimer until the time of his death. Interestingly, he had an athlete's pulse rate as well. In fact, shortly before he died, he was rejected at the Red Cross blood donor center because his pulse was below the limit. Since blood donations at the maximum permissible frequency were part of his routine, his response to the rejection was to jog up and down the stairs at his rectory just before leaving for the donations. It worked and he found it amusing to have snookered the gatekeepers at the Red Cross. But when athlete is confused with competitor, Joe's "second string" record in the tournaments might be confusing as well. Despite his talent, strength, and discipline, he could not thump his chest in victory nor blame anyone but himself in defeat. He lacked the attitudinal traits of aggression and self-promotion that may be far more important than physical prowess in the winner's circle. It's quite possible that, at least early in life, he had no awareness of this. During his high school years I got a hint of this after he returned home from an informal workout with some of his classmates on the football team. The complaint I overheard in a conversation with our parents was that he had pushed those guys all over the field, and they were first string, and he didn't make the squad. What held him back in athletic competition was, of course, the self-effacement that bordered on recklessness when it came to his own well being relative to that of others. That would ultimately get him killed, just as a variant passivity ended Milton's life as a free man.

Milton's role as the assistant was in play the night of February 24, 1987. When Teddy Simmons produced the knife after following Joe into the kitchen of the rectory and asked Joe if he believed in God, Teddy held the knife as the three marched to the rectory office and forced Joe to open the safe. And it was at Teddy's feet that Joe threw the money intended for groceries. They returned down the hallway to the kitchen. Teddy moved to cut the drapery cords until Joe stopped him and directed him to the twine in the pantry drawer, the twine that would bind him to a chair until he bled to death. (Ever the depression child, Joe abhorred waste.) They led Joe to a small room off the kitchen and tied him in a straight-backed wooden chair. As though on cue, Milton was positioned behind the chair while Teddy stood in front. Together they tied him, hastily and sloppily; they were nervous "doing" their first priest. Near the chair was a table where Joe had set the groceries he had bought to take to our mother. During the binding, they heard a noise toward the front of the house. Milton was dispatched to check. He ran past the table and struck a shopping bag knocking a can of chop suey to the floor. When he returned he picked it up but held on to it and resumed his position behind Joe's chair.

They returned to their task, but when they thought they were finished Joe raised his right arm to show a loose tie and said, "If you're going to do this, you'd better do it right." Those words, his last, still ring in my ears and contribute in large measure to my need to write this memoir. Already I have come to know my brother in much greater depth than I had in life, although I never suspected the extent of my ignorance then. This comment is at once chilling and intriguing. Intriguing because I can hear and see him in the words. It is the special role of the little brother to have heard often the mix of irritation, impatience, and even counsel that resonate in those words; they are classic Joe. Reproachful but controlled, words spoken to someone who is out of line but perhaps not beyond the reach of a hard edged reproof. I can hear the pitch, the intonation, and the touch of sarcasm. And their quotation by both boys, independently combined with their seamless fit with my memories, attest to the validity of his last words. But why?

Could he, bound in a chair with a hunting knife held inches from his eyes, have been chiding his attackers as he would have a wayward little brother? I won't ever know, but I have tested several interpretations in hopes of understanding his final moments. One is the possibility that he was trying to defuse the tension. By calling attention to the loose cord he foreclosed his last chance of escape, but perhaps the gesture would effect a time out in a scenario racing to a deadly conclusion. What mainly draws me away from that explanation is the fact that he said nothing further. He did not use the time for retying the cord to cajole, plead, or threaten. He just waited. Possibly he didn't really expect them to kill him, but he had to know. They had already robbed him at knifepoint and he was the only thing between their freedom and prison. Joe's realization of the gravity of the situation and their intent is further supported by his question to Milton, when Teddy first produced the knife in the kitchen: "Do you know what you're doing?" Milton didn't answer.

The grim interpretation, the one passing most of my tests of credibility, is that he knew his fate, was resigned to it, but could not let the moment pass without one last defiance, spoken, on its face, in taunting if not baiting words. This fits with the circumstances and is consistent with the very imprudent anger Joe displayed when instead of handing them the money from the safe, he threw it at them. Had there been any appeasing to be done, it would have started there. Still, whatever level of anger he felt might quickly have changed to panic, or at least fear, once helpless in the presence of two kids with a knife, clearly out of control of themselves but fully in control of him. Surely it is the last thing one would have expected from the young man my father worried was not tough enough to make his way in the world. But then, prudence with respect to his own well being was never part of his style. The seeming inconsistency of the man of peace and the final defiance jibes neatly with the inadvertent oxymoron of Bill Stanton who described him as both a "gentle giant" and "the most confrontational priest" he had ever known.

But, like the rest of us, gentle giants are complex. In Joe's case, Stanton's seeming contradiction may have inadvertently touched a reality beyond what most realized. Common impressions of Joe as gentle, easygoing, and infinitely patient with others' shortcomings were accurate to a point, but probably masked an anger that could have overpowered natural fear, even in the face of imminent, personal injury and death. Emotional repose settles rarely in one passionately averse to injustice and to live and work daily among the society's cast-offs is an unrelenting goad. To all appearances, a defiant, implacable anger was his final emotion. He threw the money on the floor and displayed their inept work with the twine, but he didn't fight, try to escape, or try to alert his houseguests — more than likely to avoid endangering them.

When the circumstantial case is augmented by Joe's own concern with his potential for violence, one approaches certainty. Following a posthumous award given by the Sisters of Social Service, I spoke for a while with the head of the local order who knew Joe well from the many times he had met with her and members of her community in informal discussions and more formally as a celebrant of Mass and confessor. She mentioned a conversation with Joe some time following the incident with the burglar and the fireplace poker. Joe had confided in her how disturbed he was by his behavior and the realization of his capacity and intention to inflict serious if not lethal injury. I had heard the story from Joe in my mother's apartment, but the context was the perpetrator's importunate calls from the holding center to get Joe to intercede on his behalf. The focus of the story then was not on his concern about coming within seconds of swinging the poker. If anything it was related in a casual conversation about an unpleasant incident with an unpleasant sequel. But the occasion was, as the nun told me, far more defining for Joe in his continuing efforts at turning away from violence as a response to anger. In the 1980s the Church initiated a project called Renew. I was not personally involved, but my sister attended the meetings at Joe's parish, St. Bartholomew's. She spoke recently, almost jokingly, of the night the attendees were sharing the personal issues they intended to "work on." To my sister's astonishment, Joe referred to the night with the poker as his last straw in recognizing anger as a major problem in his definition of himself as a priest and person, and why that was the target of his personal renewal. Perhaps the final irony was not only his failure to exorcise anger but to set loose its consequences ultimately upon himself.

Simmons took the advice and refastened the cord while Jones was still behind the chair. Next, Joe's shoes were pulled off and his socks stuffed into his mouth as a gag. Simmons then, at least by Jones's testimony, pulled Joe's glasses off and snapped them in half inches from Joe's then naked eyes. Tossing the glasses on the floor, Simmons gave the order to Jones and the 16-ounce chop suey can, what police called a weapon of opportunity, was driven into the top of Joe's head. The blow was delivered with enough force to crush the can across its full length into a concave crescent complementing the shape of Joe's skull. Two years later during the trial, the prosecutor, Dennis Vacco, displayed the then-rusty dented can before the jurors and spectators. To underscore the force of the blow, Vacco then held up the fragments of Joe's glasses, pointing out how both lenses had been popped from the frames from the impact. This point was at variance from Milton's version of the broken glasses, but for those watching, any impression of Milton's passivity or gentleness was effectively dispelled. This had been no tentative blow administered reluctantly to appease Simmons. The point was made to the jurors but the first impact was felt two years earlier.

Wondering what happened next prompted one of my first questions to Vacco after Joe's death: were there rope burns on his wrists or ankles? I wanted to know about signs of struggle and hence suffering during the stabbing. That was part of the larger question that took me to the State Correctional Facilities at Auburn, Attica, and Wende. What happened and why? What I learned from Milton Jones at Attica was that following the blow with the can Joe's head slumped to his chest and he appeared dazed and made no sound. Of course the gag would have muffled any words or cries. During this time Teddy Simmons stood in front of him with the knife poised for "two or three minutes" and said nothing but watched Joe intently and then began to stab him repeatedly until Joe slumped forward in the chair, his weight eventually pulling him and the chair to the floor. Milton and Teddy bolted. They were finished there.

Vacco's dramatic show with the crushed can and shattered glasses, combined with the description by Jones and Simmons of the slumping head and dazed appearance ("kind of out of it" Simmons would later say), gave some comfort to all of us who wanted to believe that Joe was unconscious during the cutting, but I have doubts. Later comments by Simmons raise doubts about the cinematic scenario of a single blow producing complete unconsciousness.

A huge part of the question prompting the visits was the savagery of an attack so far out of proportion to what was needed to steal money. Predictably, the armchair psychologists offered their thoughts almost immediately. Perhaps they had a point. In explaining the "senseless" violence, we were presented with a picture of two minority kids confronting an authority figure representing the dominant majority society. He then becomes the lightning rod for a flood of suppressed hostilities and resentments — Freud's father figure destroyed by his sons, absent the sexual motif. Knowing a bit about the sandy foundations of most theories of that ilk, and resenting any beard-stroking fatuity, especially at that time, I dismissed those pronouncements as gratuitous intrusions. But the image is compelling — the marginal street kid with a history of cadging favors from the area clergy — an angry supplicant suddenly in charge and dominating the former benefactor, who is now bound, gagged, and helpless in front of him. Then the penultimate subjugation, remove his sight. There he is, the big white priest, a popular and respected outsider, now helpless, and purblind like you. For Teddy, the glasses require no arcane symbolic interpretations. His own were outsized, very thick, heavy, and the dominant feature of his appearance, always inviting ridicule. He understood the helplessness resulting from their loss. "The Cask of Amontillado" on an east side street with all of Poe's conditions for perfect vengeance: total retribution, the victim fully aware of his fate and his executioner, and impunity from punishment. And in this case, a small profit to boot. No more humiliating stratagems to wheedle handouts from this priest on his terms. Now he had the money and the priest too.

Teddy tells it differently. Ann and I first met with him on April 14, 1992, in Auburn Correctional Facility where he had been assigned after 18 months in the Erie County Holding Center and a couple years at Elmira Correctional Facility. Auburn is the oldest prison in the New York State system, which explains its location squarely in the center of a town that grew up around it over the century since its construction. Unlike Attica, there is no spacious surrounding area; it stands along a city street where you park at a meter. The line of pickup trucks stretching across the front wall of the building clearly marks the staff parking area. In sharp contrast to Attica, the security is simple and informal, almost casual — no shoe removal or examination of my notebook for steel spiral bindings. Within ten minutes we were seated in the visitors' area, smaller than but similar in configuration to Attica.

Our assigned table was halfway down a row along one of the walls. From our position, we could observe the prisoners as they entered the hall. After waiting about 35 minutes we saw Simmons arrive, dressed in a long sleeved red shirt and tan slacks. Like Jones, he was rarely visited and clearly confused as he scanned the room several times before returning to the guards and being again pointed to our table. Still not recognizing us, he made his way along the wall, stopping at each table searching for familiar faces. Finally, he arrived in front of us, obviously taken aback. When I asked if he knew us, he nodded and sat down. I explained that we were there to learn more about Joe's murder and he agreed to discuss it with us.

His preamble was stunning — almost as if he knew the big question behind our visit. Perhaps he did. "Sometimes," he began, "you try to find something out then wish you didn't know." Then a pause as though to check on our readiness to continue. "Your brother did not die an easy death," he warned. Our reaction was a mix of despair and horror. How bad must it have been for him to acknowledge that up front? Then I realized that, while only 23, after five years behind bars he knew far more about violence and death than I, and his characterization of a hard death was no exaggeration. He had witnessed many fights in prison where the intention was to inflict injury and/or establish dominance. "You never forget that sound," he said of the wind being driven out of a man by hard blows to the body. That was the same sound he heard from the hallway as Milton Jones killed Joe. Ann and I both realized we were going to hear a totally different story in which

Simmons was only a witness.

Ted Simmons and Milton met in an East Ferry Street youth detention center in Buffalo, a facility run by the New York State Division for Youth. Having arrived before Teddy, Milton, precociously large for his age, had already become the kingpin. Shortly thereafter, Milton was transferred to Industry, N.Y., and Teddy went to Lincoln, N.Y., both state centers for delinquent youth. In the summer of 1986, they met again at Martin Luther King Park on Buffalo's east side and began spending time together. Their friendship, at least in Teddy's eyes, strengthened when Milton showed up at his house for his eighteenth birthday, February 10, 1987. As Teddy put it " I don't know if he knew it was my birthday but he was there and no one else remembered." Two weeks later their friendship would take them to Joe's house on Grider Street.

Milton had a knife he got from an uncle who lived with Milton's grandmother on Ivy Street. The man, by Teddy's description, was a bum. Milton brought the knife the night they went to Joe's "to get some money." Teddy had known Joe for several years, having stopped by the rectory numerous times to seek odd jobs for money. He believed it would arouse no suspicion on Joe's part for him to show up at the door. It didn't.

The details of entering and looting the safe were similar in Teddy's story except that the knife never left Milton's hands. In fact, when they returned from the office with Joe at knifepoint, it was Milton who began to cut the drapery cords in the room off the kitchen to use as bonds. Joe stopped him. There was no need to destroy the drapes. He showed them the pantry where a roll of twine lay in a drawer. From there they returned to the storage room off the kitchen where Teddy, following Milton's orders, began to tie Joe to the chair but deliberately tied him loosely. When Joe pointed out the loose ties, Teddy, again at Milton's direction, refastened them securely.

Somehow Teddy placed himself in the alley outside when the killing commenced. It was from there he heard the now familiar sounds of the beating and stabbing. But he knew about the glasses. His version corroborated and perhaps formed the basis of Dennis Vacco's dramatic representation to the courtroom. The glasses, according to Teddy, were knocked from Joe's face by the force of the can striking his head then broken when Milton stepped on them. The storage room is not visible from the outside, so the veracity of Teddy's selective observation is questionable.

They left the rectory by the side door and cut through the Church parking lot to the street behind and parallel to Grider. Neither of them returned and they saw no one. In neither version do they meet the young man on Grider Street who told police of seeing a young black man about 5'6" in height running from the rectory clutching something under a jacket. At the trial he recognized Milton's line up photo and pointed out the 6'4" Jones in the courtroom as the man he had seen that night. At the time of his statement to the police, he had been charged with another crime.

Teddy sat at the table and spoke softly and articulately about the events of that night. His response to the inconsistencies pointed out repeatedly by Ann were often less than believable but spoken with an unswerving consistency in support of his relative innocence in the whole business. Yes, he stole and that was wrong, but the violent part was neither his idea nor doing. He was, as the trial defense alleged, coerced by Milton who had threatened to hurt someone in his family if he didn't cooperate. Simmons was, after all, always quiet, shy, and not into violence. A few things about him lent credence to that self-description.

Simmons is of average height, but thin. His fingernails were gnawed to the quick and it was clear that survival for him in prison was a struggle. Because of his exemplary good behavior he was assigned to "honors company" at Auburn. Members of this company were segregated in a special cellblock where they enjoyed certain privileges as rewards for demonstrated cooperation. Simmons's job at Auburn was running an elevator. While there he had completed an associate's degree from Onondaga Community College in Syracuse. He avoided the general population which was dangerous anyway, but especially for him since some former fellow inmates from the Erie County Holding Center were also there and spread the word that he had killed two priests. When not working, he spent most of his time in his single bed cell reading. By his count he had read two thousand books since incarceration there and depended on interlibrary loans because of the limited library at Auburn. Books he favored were in the sciences, especially biology. He also read quite a few comic books, he added with a smile.

Earlier in his incarceration at Auburn, he had been in "more fights than I can count." That's something you have to do or the wolf packs will own you. You become their personal vassals, fully at their disposal for errands, money, and sex. To avoid that and be left alone and respected you need to prove that you'll fight. Simmons's tales of countless fights was difficult to square with his physical size. Intimidation is the political system among prisoners and between them and the guards. For many, violence was a way of life before arriving and a reason for it. Add to that the absence of any personal protections or rights, and physical aggressiveness and muscle rise to the top of prerequisites for status in the pecking order and, beyond that, survival. Teddy, by the time of our visit, had long retreated from even recreational sports in prison. He had enjoyed playing basketball as a kid and had, in fact, played often at the school gym at St. Bart's. Basketball at Auburn, however, was only a format for combat. Broken bones, gouged eyes and loosened teeth, were the order of the day on the courts, so he stayed away. While on the street as a kid he had been abused about his scrawny build, thick glasses, and reputation as a loner. In his description of his first meeting with Milton at the detention center, one catches a clear sense of Teddy's attraction to a companion who could complement or compensate for his own lack of physical prowess.

After their apprehension, it was generally believed that Teddy was the mind and Milton the muscle. Nothing about Teddy's appearance, manner, or circumstances at Auburn argued against that impression. A review of the scenario easily drew Milton as the slow-witted passive partner who committed his violence on command but not with the explosive savagery characteristic of both murders. That dimension, according to prevailing wisdom before and during the trials, was the mark of the seething rage of an east side kid for whom disrespect, the ultimate evil, was a steady diet.

During Milton Jones's trial, the defense attempted to establish that Milton had been an accomplice under duress. The reasoning was that Teddy Simmons had threatened to harm Milton's family unless he complied. Dennis Vacco, the assistant district attorney prosecuting the first trial, rebutted that argument by underscoring the physical differences between Jones and Simmons; the latter, spindly with poor eyesight aided by noticeably thick glasses, and Jones, a tall 6' 4" heavily built young man who had played football in high school (a gentle, tractable kid according to the coach). Simmons's lack of physical strength was also reflected in a mocking sobriquet used by his peers in school and the neighborhood. Vacco's attempt to slip that into the record was blocked by the judge. But it was clear from appearances, testimony, and Simmons's own later comments that he had been the object of extensive abuse while growing up in the cruel world of children. What we read about the frustrated, powerless minority kid lashing out against the big powerful authority figure was a fairly plausible hypothesis under the circumstances and at the time.

This was 12 years before Columbine, a word that has entered our national consciousness as a symbol and synonym for deadly rage, presumably caused by rejection, abuse, and psychological bullying by peers. At the small, quiet town of Littleton, Colorado, on April 20, 1999, two students arrived at their high school with explosives and high powered weapons to execute a well prepared plan to wipe out a substantial portion of the student body, eventually to include themselves. Among the myriad consequences of this staggering event was a closer look at the realities of the adolescent (and earlier) culture, where failure to fit in is tantamount to endless days of emotional and often physical assault. The occasional reactions to this had never reached the scale of the Columbine attack where 14 students and one teacher were shot to death, many at close range, in a rampage of hatred that is often attributed to the cumulative resentment of peer rejection. Five years after the killings, a follow up investigation was released that disputed the bullying hypothesis, but still the issue was underscored, causing widespread appreciation of the ubiquity and pain of rejection, especially in the adolescent world.

The armchair psychologists in the "priest murders" did not have the Columbine killings for a model, or they might well have cited rejection and bullying to explain the behavior, and they might have had a point. Teddy Simmons was a loner who lacked even family support. To what extent the savagery of the murders could be explained by a lifetime of resentment and suppressed anger cannot be known, even by him, but when interviewed, he emphasized the importance of not picking on the kid who is not handsome, athletic, and popular among his peers. Was Simmons the powder keg of resentment and rage that results from growing up disdained and rejected by everyone who matters, and in his case, apparently everyone? Could the wanton violence of the attacks have been his Columbine syndrome? More curiosity about his perception of reality arises from the lengthy, self-incriminating revelations he made to his police escorts in the plane back from San Diego. Included in the information he volunteered was that both priests had recognized him as fellow victim of Milton Jones's rampage and appealed to Milton to spare him. That story did not reappear in his confession, at any point in the trial, or in our conversations at the prison. He was clearly embellishing the version of unwilling accomplice apparently believing the alleged identification with the victims would follow him into the justice system.

Was this young man so victimized by peers and adults that he believed his retaliation would be condoned and even forgiven once understood by an accepting authority figure? The trial testimony of the escorting officers made clear that they were actually surprised by the flood of his "confessions" to them and had advised him at the outset of his right to remain silent. But he insisted he had to tell someone, which he did all the way from San Diego to Buffalo. Given the fact that his disclosures were preposterous incriminations of Milton and vindications of himself, his need to "unburden" himself is clear. Still, the gratuitous savagery of the murders remains a mystery if the scenario of an opportunistic robbery stands alone. One is reminded of Joe's description of Teddy as unstable and Teddy's self-description as a nerd appearing several times in his statements; references always linked to his large thick glasses.

Theodore Simmons following guilty verdict, September 23, 1988. Photo by Ronald J. Colleran, *Buffalo News* file photo

Looking across the table at this spidery thin young man who speaks directly and credibly of his insulation from the wolf pack environment in the general prison population, one begins to wonder. From the time of his arrest in San Diego, he consistently denied any direct participation in the beating and stabbing of Joe or Monsitgnor Herlihy. Setting aside the theory of the police and DA's office that depicted Milton as the stooge and Teddy as the instigator, one begins to consider the conflicting stories on the basis of what facts stand without interpretation: 1) Milton Jones had been sent to detention as a teenager for hitting another boy with a pipe in a dispute over a bicycle; 2) Milton admitted at the time of his arrest and during our conversation to hitting both Joe and Monsignor Herlihy. The force of those blows was intentional and sufficient to inflict serious injury and perhaps kill; 3) During the intervening ten days between the attacks, Milton was discovered by a friend sharpening the knife on an electric grinding wheel in his room (The knife, a hunting knife estimated to have a four and one half inch blade, has never been found.); 4) In his statements to the police, Milton admitted to stabbing each of the victims "only once"; 5) To the best of anyone's knowledge, Teddy Simmons was not violent. The exception is his own assertion of having been in "more fights than I can count" after first arriving at Auburn. A cursory observation of Teddy's physical size relative to other inmates of the general population renders that assertion suspect. (At the time of his arrest in 1987, he reported himself as 5' 11" tall weighing 170 pounds.) But it appears being cool and tough was important to Teddy. In the early years of their imprisonment, he and Jones exchanged some notes and Teddy described himself as "chilling out" at Auburn.

In the context of these realities, Simmons's disavowal of an active role in the beatings is consistent and believable. But you don't believe him easily. During the recounting of the events, his affect shows little or no emotion. His most palpable emotions during the conversation were a sigh that seemed to come from his toes when he reflected on his sentence, exclaiming, "fifty years!" and his description of being haunted by the sounds of men being beaten in prison. Some hint of his credibility and sensitivity may also be gleaned from his answer to a friend who asked him after the Herlihy murder about the paper bag full of money stolen from St. Matthew's — "I'm a businessman." His credibility is diminished further by his consistent and inventive efforts to lay the entire fault on Milton. In his statements to the San Diego police, who arrested him at 3:00 a.m. the morning after Monsignor Herlihy's murder, he immediately characterized his involvement as minimal — participating only because of Milton's threat to kill his mother and uninvolved in physical violence to either victim. In fact, he witnessed the murder of Joe from an outside window after Milton had finished stabbing him. When offering that information, Teddy would not have known his fingerprint would be lifted from the cash box in Joe's office where the three of them went when Joe was quite alive. When refusing to enter the residence of Monsignor Herlihy, Teddy was threatened by Milton with a .357 magnum and complied out of fear of his life. Indeed, Teddy had attempted in both cases to stop Milton from harming either priest and even depicted himself in a "good thief" role, allied with the victims against Milton's unstoppable murderous course. In Teddy's statement to the San Diego and Buffalo police, we see both priests immediately recognizing Teddy's victim status and even urging him to spare himself from Milton's wrath by cooperating. Joe, according to Teddy, told him to do what Milton said, since there was no point in both of them being killed, and Monsignor Herlihy invited him to stay the night after being ordered by Milton to tell the priest he had no place to sleep. Teddy was even stepping in front of Milton to protect the priests but was overpowered.

A number of people believe that Joe forgave the boys before they killed him. I am uncertain of the source of that belief, but it may well have come from these statements of Teddy in which he portrays both priests as grateful for his courage in trying to halt the out-of-control Milton Jones. The inconsistency of this story with his being physically absent from the room where Milton alone killed Joe is one of the factors that tips the credibility edge to Milton. Milton has never denied his culpability except in the one letter where he appeared less than fully lucid. And Milton, too, expressed in one of his letters to me a remark indicative of a history of rejection and betrayal consistent with a Columbine explanation: "I was always made fun of by people who said they were my friends, and I was always hurt." The timing of that statement is important in its interpretation. Written years later after experiencing the harsh conditions of a maximum security prison, it could well have been a recollection retrofitted with the abuses he endured in prison. We can't know. Beyond this, for me there is something telling and intriguing about Teddy's glasses and the murders. They are the arresting feature of his appearance and certainly a major reason for his characterization by himself and others as a nerd. Their effect may be more profound than we can imagine.

Eyes enter disproportionately into Teddy's role in the murders. I recall clearly my first conversation with Milton in 1992, when he described Teddy's behavior. When Joe was securely bound and gagged in the chair, Teddy pulled Joe's glasses off and snapped them in half in front of his face. After Milton struck with the food can, Teddy stared into Joe's face for "several minutes" before the stabbing began. In Teddy's statements to police, the eye motif appears twice more, both times in Teddy's version of Milton's actions. In Teddy's statement about Monsignor Herlihy's killing, he describes Milton as hitting the priest then ordering him (Teddy) to "sit in front of the priest and look in his eyes." During his lengthy narrative in the plane en route from San Diego, Teddy told the detectives that after Joe was tied and gagged, "Milton looks directly into the priest's eyes and stabs the priest in the neck area." Were Teddy's weak eyes and their extensive consequences for his status on the street something of an obsession? Might he have concentrated all of his frustrations and rage into the features accounting for his "nerd" status? I can only speculate, but in my mind those oversized glasses played a major role in the savage death of two innocent men.

Those facts, the few we have, still don't fit with the impressions of the two boys. Simmons's appearance, manner, and obvious intelligence suggest a solitary, calculating, and manipulative person. This is reinforced by Joe's strong uneasiness in his presence and characterization of him as "unstable." This was at a point in his life when Joe had extensive experience with young people, many of whom were not model citizens. Milton, by contrast, seems open, spontaneous, and very remorseful. High school classmates had described him as a "Teddy Bear" and his demeanor fits. Of course, if the facts we have do tell the story, Milton should be remorseful and Teddy guilty only of burglary and allegedly acting under duress, is appropriately remorseful for his 50-year sentence.

Rashomon was a cult film I first saw in 1964 at Washington, D.C.'s then one and only art theater. Set in medieval Japan, it depicts an assault seen in reiterations by the victim, the guard, the attacker, and the victim's husband. As Teddy and Milton point to one another as the real villain, I am reminded of the compelling (if tedious) lesson of *Rashomon* of how a single event is perceived very differently by the participants to a point where those perceptions in time become the truth, leaving whatever we consider objective reality forever in question. In this case, dependent on the testimony and recall of persons highly motivated to lie, we are left for our truth with physical evidence, witness testimony, points of

Standing during sentencing on November 1, 1988, from left are defendant Milton Jones and his attorneys, Jeffrey A. Sellers and John J. Carney III; George R. Blair, defense attorney for Theodore Simmons; and defendant Theodore Simmons — others unidentified. Photo by Richard W. Roeller. *Buffalo News* file photo.

convergence in the perpetrators' reports, assumptions based on circumstances, and our knowledge of the persons involved. We will never know all the details of who did what, when, or how often, but the murder of Monsignor Herlihy ten days later lays to rest any question about an isolated event where two otherwise harmless young men were caught up in an unplanned incident that spun out of control.

Recounting the details of that night brings to the fore a question about Joe's judgment, a question that harks back to some of my memories of him as a young man. On the third anniversary of his death, following a Mass at the Buffalo State College Newman Center, a crowd gathered in the community room and began exchanging stories about Joe. I told one about hiding in the closet of our bedroom while he was in the bathroom grooming himself for his Saturday night date and singing at the top of his lungs. He was in his senior year at Canisius College and I was still in high school. When he finally emerged from his ablutions and pulled open the closet door, I lunged forward from the shadows. The shock and surprise were better than I could have expected, so successful, in fact that I had to try again the next week. That second night, *The Mikado* (that year's Glee Club musical) songs seemed especially exuberant but endless as I lay curled behind the clothes. But finally, the doors were yanked open and there he was, naked and vulnerable. Again I lunged and growled and he began to recoil as expected, but suddenly, while the first peals of laughter were still in my throat, I was slammed against the closet wall driven by a bare foot that caught me squarely in the chest. It was the second and final episode in an abbreviated series of "let's scare Joe to death" stunts. Had he been wearing shoes the ending would have been far worse for me.

I told the story then and retell it now to underscore a difference between us and a characteristic of Joe's that bears on his life as well as that last night. He learned from his mistakes. But if you believe that, and I do, how do you explain the obvious "foolishness" of his behavior that night? Two boys appear at his door, one unknown and very large, the other known and very unnerving, "unstable" as he put it. Was I wrong about his capacity to learn? On the surface, it might appear so, but that level masks an essential distinction. Where Joe and I were similar was in frequently acting contrary to the dictates of good judgment. Where for me it was often because of impatience or self-seeking, for him it was an affirmative imprudence that informed his adult life. He knew the path of good judgment and prudence but chose often not to follow it. From what point in his life this began I don't know, but it was announced the weekend of his ordination when he made it clear who would be his career model. He would subordinate security and personal comfort for what he believed to be his vocation.

The issue of prudence was central to his life and death. It emerged for me as I was struggling with a memorial observation for the tenth anniversary of his death. I used it in a radio commentary on WBFO, the regional NPR station, and again, slightly modified, in a reflection for the Bishop's Mass at the Cathedral where Joe and

Monsignor Herlihy were remembered. The remarks overlap much of what has been said earlier but serve as a fitting recapitulation of Joe — a man whose quixotic quest for fairness was masked to most by his demeanor as a high-spirited, open-minded, and easy-going priest.

> Ten years ago this month my brother was murdered by two young men who arrived at his door claiming to be hungry and without a place to stay. He was making them baloney sandwiches when the knife appeared. Joe was a priest who had spent most of his career living and working among the poor, often in neighborhoods where prudent people did not open their doors to strangers at night. That night a little prudence could have prevented a violent death to a man devoted to peace.
>
> But prudence was not what his life was about. The day he was ordained, he spoke of his commitment to follow the path of another who long ago met a savage death for his lack of prudence. Joe was not grandiose about that commitment but he was serious. He knew that his choice would take him into the wind, but he persisted quietly and deliberately without a sign of reproach to the majority of us who opted for prudence over principle, especially when the latter was risky.
>
> In the early 1980s, troubled deeply by the massive increase in our defense budget he protested by withholding a proportionate amount of his taxes. He explained this to the IRS in a letter and also to his parishioners from the pulpit and in the

church bulletin. This was not a prudent move. I worried that he was inviting trouble but it passed quietly and only after his death did I find among his papers a precise accounting of the amount he withheld, every dollar of which was donated to organizations working for peace and nuclear disarmament.

After his death the IRS appeared again looking for $36 they believed he owed from his last tax return. While looking for the $36 I uncovered another example of imprudence. In 1986 he had taken a salary from his parish of $2700. He had made provision for the basics of a very basic life but no provisions whatsoever for retirement or any other personal security.

I visited his killers in prison a couple times and learned that he had two final opportunities for prudence the night he died. When forced to open the safe he threw the money at the men, and after he was tied in a chair he raised an arm to show a loosely fastened cord, saying as he did, "If you're going to do this, you'd better do it right."

In today's idiom it would be said he walked the walk — meaning that his beliefs, words, and actions were all cut from the same cloth. It is the fundamental meaning of integrity, but not an integrity by default. Joe knew exactly what he was doing. He entered the priesthood to devote his life to those whose need was greatest. But he was no bloodless ascetic. He loved a cold beer and a warm fire as much as any of us but he could not savor those pleasures fully while others were cold and thirsty. A prudent man could have.

And so I reflect on a life of generosity and principle in a time when we seem to celebrate self above all else and integrity in public life appears an aberration. To paraphrase an old question, "If living our lives according to our religious or moral beliefs were against the law, would any of us be arrested?"

WBFO commentary, 25 Feb 1997

Raymond P. Bissonette, brother of the slain Rev. A. Joseph Bissonette, confers with his wife Ann, during the trial of Milton Jones and Theodore Simmons. Daughter, Marya, is at right. Photo by Dennis Enser. *Buffalo News* file photo.

CHAPTER EIGHTEEN

DON'T YOU WISH THEY'D FRY?

One of the frequent commiserations offered to me and others in my family following the arrest and again after the trials concerned our presumed frustration that the death penalty in New York State had been outlawed. For me it was no disappointment at all, but not for any lofty or humanitarian reasons; to the contrary, I considered it too easy in view of the suffering they had inflicted on their victims and countless others connected to them. In my mind at the time, a swift, comparatively painless death was grossly out of proportion to the gruesomeness of what they did. I have never seen the death penalty as the ultimate in terms of eye-for-an-eye justice.

But subsequent events would change my thinking on all counts. Following the election of Governor George Pataki, capital punishment was reinstated. That was 1995, eight years after the murders and six years after the last trial. The murders were still part of our region's collective memory, and I was asked a number of times to comment. As typically happens, the expectation of an audience prompts some reflection on the subject. My reflection exposed a void. In researching the issue, I came to appreciate the factual basis of the opponents of capital punishment and the special appeal of those facts to people like Joe who were disposed thematically to find class-based distinctions in any dimension of life opportunity objectionable.

After stumbling through a variety of forums in which I attempted to articulate my new thoughts on the subject, I developed a rationale that began to make sense. What became a fairly coherent position that I think reflects what Joe believed, and what I came to believe about the issue as it applied to him, evolved over the years from 1995 through 1997. It has only been reinforced by my experience with Joe's killers and observing the increasing frequency of DNA-based conviction reversals for capital crimes and other felonies. The following remarks, prepared for delivery in December of 1997, contain the substance of my reasoning then and now.

> Sister Helen Prejean, whose death row ministry inspired the film, *Dead Man Walking*, recently spoke in Buffalo. Her visit and the trial of Timothy McVeigh, an area native, have heightened

consciousness regionally about the death penalty.

Having lost a brother to murder, I too have been thinking and fielding questions about it lately. One result has been a realization that at the time of my brother's death, my views on capital punishment were ill-informed at best. At the time I was not, like my brother, opposed to capital punishment; in fact I regarded it as almost merciful, compared with lingering death in a cage. I still think so, but for other reasons have shifted strongly in the direction of those who oppose it on principle.

We don't like to be reminded, but our legal system is no less subject to human failure than our other institutions. The ugly reality is that we do punish innocent people. We learn with disturbing frequency of prisoners set free sometimes after years of incarceration. For every one of them there are others whose cases don't get that second look. That incredibly joyous return to freedom will never follow an execution. We know of 23 cases of innocent people put to death — not a big number unless you're one of them. We also know of 73 people released from death row since 1973 after evidence emerged that proved them innocent. Just this December a meeting was held in Toronto attended by nine Americans and Canadians imprisoned and later discovered to be innocent. One had been in prison for 23 years. And because we know of those numbers we know they aren't the total, only that it's bigger and always too big.

Some think we go too far protecting the rights of

the accused. Sometimes I agree but then I wonder how many unpunished criminals justify the horror of one innocent man jailed or hanged.
For me it's a lot. We should move mountains to prevent that. I am stunned by the mindset reflected in an assertion attributed to a former Virginia attorney general that subsequent evidence of innocence is irrelevant if a fair trial was conducted.

Sentiment aside, the death penalty doesn't work. It may make us feel vindicated but it doesn't do what we like to think justifies it rationally — deter others from similar acts. That belief is ancient. We read in Deuteronomy the simple rationale — " the people shall see and be afraid." Back then it might have been true but nobody really sees anymore, and the fear deters only those who expect to be caught. Beyond that, is the death penalty that much more inhibiting than life behind bars? An eighteenth century philosopher, Cesare Beccaria, argued that, unlike death, which is soon forgotten, a life sentence would be a greater deterrent because of the continuing reminder of the crime and its perpetrator. And in our time, after hundreds of studies, the evidence for a deterrent effect just isn't there. Instead of evidence we have, as Monsignor David Gallivan (nephew of the late Monsignor David Herlihy) said in a recent parish bulletin, politicians framing the argument as though the only two alternatives are a revolving prison door or the noose.

What the evidence does show, however, is a death row populated mostly by the poor, the powerless, and minorities — often all three. The data are

> extensive and compelling but for race one statistic tells the story — in 65 years only one white person has been executed for the murder of a black person. And as for wealth, justice may not be for sale but neither is money irrelevant. In the words of Bourke Corcoran, an American politician who died in 1923, too early to watch the Simpson trial, — "You simply cannot hang a millionaire in America."
>
> And so ten years after killing my brother, his killers are alive and it doesn't worry me. I wonder often what he would think.

Now I wonder less about what he would think. Consistent with what he felt about the intruder in his home, he would have expected and wanted not a slap on the wrist but an appropriate punishment. Moreover, he would not have presumed to forgive the killer of Monsignor Herlihy. But I do believe that about now he would say "enough." The number of years in a sentence is highly relative in reality. Prison life is vastly different depending on the institution and your position in the hierarchy. Even today, priest killers are targets of "special" attention by staff and other inmates. Equivalencies of time and degree of suffering are impossible to measure with any accuracy, but there is no question that a year in a maximum security prison housed with what those in the business call "the worst of the worst" is far longer than a year in low security detention center. And even prisons of comparable security level vary greatly in the severity of life on the inside. Attica, in anyone's book, is hard time.

Mary Bissonette attends a memorial service for her son on the first anniversary of his death. The service was held at St. Joseph's Church on February 24, 1988. Photo by James P. McCoy. *Buffalo News* file photo.

CHAPTER NINETEEN

THE BUTTERFLY'S WINGS

In chaos theory one learns about the butterfly in Colorado whose fluttering wings begin a chain of events ending a month later in a cyclone in Indonesia. These apparently random and distorted interconnections in time and place obtain in this story as well. I refer in particular to two recent conditions with special relevance. First are the convulsions in the Church resulting from the alleged and confirmed sexual (usually homosexual) predation by priests on children. Second is the present state of one of Joe's killers. Were this a newspaper or magazine report, the former would be a sidebar. The latter, in this case, offers a tragic aspect of the conclusion and an irony relative to the theme of this narrative.

Just after the trials in 1988 I went to Nepal where I spent some time along the Bagmati River observing burial and purification customs at a shrine called Pashupati. I was more than a little astonished at having encountered that word for the second time in my life in environments and contexts so far removed in space and time.

Swami Pashupati, self-described as pastor of Mother Serapi's Church of the Holy Quietness, made his appearance the day after Joe was killed. From his apartment in North Tonawanda, a community close to Buffalo, he called Florida to reach an acquaintance who had been a reporter for one of our local TV stations, Channel 7. The purpose of the Swami's call was to inform her that the priest killed the night before was one of his "clients," whom he had been counseling about romantic relationships with young black males. She, along with almost everyone else, was suspicious of his motives in calling her rather than the police and reported the call to the Buffalo police. In their follow up investigation, they found a man with multiple sclerosis living with his brother in an apartment in North Tonawanda that doubled as his home and gathering place for the ten or twelve disciples of Mother Serapi. After investigating, the police dismissed him as an opportunist ("crackpot" in their idiom) attempting to capitalize on a high visibility case. But the call and report became part of the record. As the trial approached, it became potentially incendiary. Both Joe's and Monsignor Herlihy's murders were singularly savage, giving rise to all manner of speculation about drugs and other triggers for such rage on the part of the killers. A homosexual relationship gone bad was surely among them, although not expressed publicly. Moreover, the defense attorneys had used the fear of fanning such beliefs as a lever to gain a plea bargain in return for sparing the families of the victims and the Diocese the risk of embarrassment. Vacco, as part of his very thorough approach to prosecuting the case, called a meeting on a Saturday morning for all interested parties. Our family, the Herlihys, representatives of the Bishop, and attorneys for the Buffalo Catholic Diocese all were present. In all there were probably thirty people in the room.

Vacco explained the report, the conclusions of the investigation, and his assessment of the likelihood of the Swami's allegation surfacing at trial. Legally it had no relevance as a defense, but if even mentioned, a media frenzy would follow and reputations would suffer irreparably. Following his presentation, the sentiment was unanimous to go forward with the trial and reject any plea deal regardless of the risk.

We all felt good about the decision, especially its immediate unanimity. But later, Ann and I began to wonder about whether Joe's reputation was still too much at risk. We were both adamantly committed to prevent some malicious publicity seeking from destroying all that remained of Joe — his memory and reputation. The probability of the report's reaching the public domain was tiny, but the consequences were, in our view, disproportionately immense. Public awareness of homosexuality among the clergy was high even then, and the Swami's allegation would have played dramatically into the widespread suspicions already out there, especially given the nature of the crimes. After extensive worry and discussion, we agreed to a preemptive move to minimize or bury the risk of this story's reaching the public through the media. We knew that, once out, it would take on a life of its own, defying any evidence contrary to the initial impressions, especially a story satisfying existing suspicions and so readily suited to resolve the ghastly circumstances. Moreover, it would live forever, rekindled and exaggerated by every suspected or actual misdeed by a Catholic priest. Of course, at the time we had no idea how right we were. Joe's death would have become an endlessly reverberating, "I told you so."

Our plan had two parts: conduct our own investigation of the Swami's story and then present our findings to the television stations and newspaper, so that if the report came out they would have the facts first before reporting an unsubstantiated bid for attention that would irreversibly damage Joe's reputation in the minds of countless people.

We began. The Swami had described Joe as a big blond priest who wore blue jeans and a medallion engraved with the words "I am a Priest." Despite worrying about the situation, we chuckled at the idea of Joe's sporting a medallion. And neither of us had ever seen him in blue jeans. We joked that he must have had a special wardrobe dedicated to his counseling sessions. (The wry smile reappeared the day we cleared out his apartment and found no blue jeans.) But the Swami, to bolster his claims, had named other people in the community who could presumably back up his story or lend credibility to it or him. We chased those people down, in several cases having to do step-by-step networking to find people no longer in the area. It was a difficult and somewhat frantic process, but in time we had the documentation we needed. Ann had carefully taken notes of every conversation with names and dates. She consolidated the information into a single detailed report intended for use as a resource in our conversations with the media people. Then we commenced step two: in-person meetings with management of the three TV channels and *The Buffalo News*.

Our first appointment was with the news director of Channel 7. We started there because we both thought it to have an aggressive and somewhat sensational style, focusing on local news. We were well received and given a very courteous and patient hearing. We supplied copies of our "findings" and reviewed every point in detail. Of course, there and elsewhere we strongly underscored the purpose of all this and openly acknowledged that once we told them what we knew, which was far more than what was in the police files, we were at their mercy. But the interest of Channel 7 was more than either of us anticipated. After our first meeting to present our case, I was asked to present the material on tape. Acutely aware that I was providing fuel for my own immolation and Joe's, I agreed and spent close to two hours on camera. It was a long and grueling day but I welcomed the opportunity in the perhaps naïve confidence that our disclosure would be respected in proportion to its openness and detail.

We continued on our way, ending a very busy week on a Friday afternoon in the offices of Murray Light, then the managing editor of *The Buffalo News.* That interview had a different feel. Both Ann and I sensed an atmosphere that was not hostile but somewhat adversarial and certainly not as sympathetic to our goal as the reception at the TV stations. Part way into our meeting, Light brought a young man into the office whom he introduced as Stan Evans, his new associate editor. Both listened, but asked few questions and, by comparison with the TV people, conveyed a noticeable sense of impatience. It could easily have been a Friday afternoon effect, but I soon learned an alternative explanation. It came at nine the next morning with a call from Mr. Evans who had a grand idea to spike any future rumors by running a special front page story the following day, Sunday!

Initially I felt we had failed to make ourselves clear, until I realized the splash he could make with that story all over the front page of the Sunday edition. It wasn't difficult to imagine the headline. At the time I was off guard, but realized quickly enough that his preemptive story would totally defeat our preemptive story. I thanked him for his interest and politely declined. We were angered by what we saw as an opportunistic effort to capitalize on what we considered a binding gentlemen's agreement. It brought sharply to the surface the very risk we agonized over when considering insinuating ourselves in the first place. But we were grateful that he asked. He had no legal obligation to do so and honored our request to drop the idea. Nonetheless, he felt compelled to take a shot at releasing himself from his "seal of confession" by convincing me his plan would serve our purposes. We were ingenuous enough to believe respect for Joe and the circumstances of his death would outweigh the prospect of selling out every paper in Western New York. And we were right.

After that we thought it was over until an investigative reporter from Channel 7 called the next week. He had already found photographs of several large blond priests in the Diocese and been to the Swami's apartment to test his recall of the troubled priest. He asked to come over and I agreed. He showed me the pictures and pointed out the person the Swami had misidentified initially, but then on a second try, correctly identified Joe. How he could have missed in the first place is surprising. By that time Joe's picture had been in the paper and on all three TV channels at least a dozen times in all. But I was impressed by the resourcefulness of the reporter, and there would be more. He arrived with a camera crew and soon we were in my living room listening to me trying to respond to a pretty penetrating interrogation which included as a final question, asked very dramatically in anticipation of future airing: "How do you know your brother is not gay?" I fumbled with the answer and was angry with myself, but, unlike most situations of that kind, the "perfect" answer did not take form, as it often does, some time later. In this case, not the next minute nor the next year. I still don't know how I could have responded with anything definitive, any more than I could have had he asked about my mother, my wife, or my kids. By then Channel 7 had enough tape for a mini series and I had given it to them. But the issue was never broached and still remains buried with Joe.

The Swami's moment of glory slipped away, but some years later I learned he had been appointed the Hindu chaplain at the Buffalo campus of the State University. I was enraged and scheduled a meeting with the head of the chaplains, a young, amiable Lutheran minister named Roger Ruff. Ann and I met him for breakfast and told him why we considered the Swami unfit for such a position. He was sympathetic but clearly not inclined to make any changes, and noted the Swami's apparent mastery of the Hindu religion. He also made reference to some maltreatment of him by a Catholic priest who had allegedly pushed him down some stairs. I would have given a great deal to learn who that was but never did. But, for whatever reason, his tenure as chaplain was short lived as, I soon learned, he was also.

CHAPTER TWENTY

REHABILITATION?

At the time of our initial visit to Milton Jones, he had been imprisoned for five years. Nearly two had been spent in the Erie County Holding Center awaiting trial and three more at Attica, a maximum security prison that gained national attention in 1972 for a lengthy and bloody uprising. Attica is a place for serious, and often violent, offenders. Built like a fortress, it rises to dominate a sparsely-populated, semi-rural community in Western New York. Its clean stucco appearance is disarmingly attractive and benign until you enter and find a massive human warehouse where fear, suspicion, and brutality are the central features of the environment for staff and inmates alike.

Learning of Milton's initial experiences of physical assault by the guards (corrections officers) was unsettling. But by the time of our visit, it appeared his life had settled into a dull but relatively non-threatening routine. Had that been the case, it was not to last. Subsequent letters to me and reports from Sister Karen reveal a seeming unrelenting history of attacks by guards and other inmates. Jail time for certain types of crime is especially hard. You are an outcast and target of both the keepers and the kept. From his descriptions, it appears some of the violence may also have been due to his refusal to yield to certain norms of the inmate culture. For example, he was once ordered by other inmates not to use the phone in the yard. He insisted to me that he was entitled to the phone and apparently said something similar to whoever warned him off. The result was a severe beating with a metal pipe that broke his nose and jaw, loosened his teeth, and cut his face. Ironically, his surgery was at Erie County Medical Center, across the street from Joe's former rectory.

In one letter he refers to pressures to engage in homosexual acts that he resisted. The litany of his mistreatment is detailed in literally blow-by-blow fashion in his letters to me, in which he names names and details the events. Typically, the abuses and his reaction to them are referenced to Muslim and Christian scripture where he quotes passages related to mistreatment of Mohammed, Christ, and their followers. Ironically, with regard to scripture, the chronicle reminds me of the story of Job. Where there may be elements of self-pity, he is more than entitled to it. More interesting, however, are his struggles to make sense of his circumstances in the context of the religious teachings contained in the scriptures he has obviously read in great detail.

The resurgence of attacks in recent years seems exacerbated by limited if not absent social support from any quarter. In a letter a few years ago, in which the censor redacted the date but left in the names of the attackers Milton names, he begins with a seemingly cheery salutation introducing six pages chronicling abusive treatment, even predating his arrest. After the salutation he relates a history of betrayal and ridicule dating back to his childhood, followed by a litany of mistreatment at the hands of guards and prisoners. Toward the end, perhaps in anticipation of a suicide attempt in which he cut his wrist with a shard of broken lens from his glasses, he (again with the scriptural reference) states that he has decided to die "... for the redemption of the sins and wrongdoings of my family and friends."

The next letter gave me reason to believe that he had been driven over the edge and his mind had snapped. It was written in September 2003. From the very start it is different. In a letter a year earlier, he had begun in his usual fashion, inquiring about the well being of me and family members, always named individually, and addressing me by my first name. In the September letter, however, the salutation is "Dear Dr. Bissonette." After that he alludes to the Hippocratic oath (he knows I am on the faculty of the medical school and apparently assumes I am a physician) and then, writing about himself in the third person and using his prison number in every self reference, he asks for a prayer for himself with scriptural quotations as rationale. The wording he provides for the requested prayer is quoted here in part:

> Dear Lord God I beseech thee on behalf of Milton Jones who is incarcerated and whose identification number is 88-B-2329, and the prayer that I'm praying to you for on his behalf is as follows: we as Christians who are in authoritative positions and non-authoritative positions, and who uphold the law of the land as well as the Holy Bible when it suits our purposes know that Milton Jones 88-B-2329 has been accused and convicted of the death and murder of Father A. Joseph Bissonette and Monsignor David Herlihy who are two Catholic priests from Buffalo, New York, who is now and has been for some time under the care and custody of the Department of Correctional Services within the New York …

The prayer continues for four more pages and the letter ends "Thank you Ray for the prayer. God speed."

The prayer is replete with assertions of victimization, both psychological and physical, but contains elements different from previous letters and personal conversations: there is a dissociative quality to the third person point of view and the constant pairing of his name with his prison number, and, for the first time he actually asserts innocence of the murders. Convinced that he was no longer fully rational, I wrote a brief reply agreeing to pray for him. Then my letter was returned with a note on the envelope that read "released." His "release," I learned from Sister Karen, was to a mental health treatment facility within the prison system from which he was transferred to Wende where Karen and I went in May.

Both of us expected the worst. We were placed at a table in the visitor area and, presently, he arrived. I had not seen him in twelve years but his gait and appearance, despite a weight gain of fifty pounds, were unmistakable. He approached our table and sat down, seeming relaxed and comfortable. To our surprise, he also seemed fully rational and in touch. Following his transfer from Attica for treatment, he had been freed from the stresses of that environment and put on a course of medication that seemed to have been effective in relieving his symptoms but causing a rapid weight gain. I explained that I was trying to write a story of Joe's life and wanted to speak to him one more time before completing the first draft. Specifically, I wondered if he knew anything more about the murders that might have been overlooked before. The short answer to that question was "no" and so the conversation turned to his circumstances and recovery.

The conversation did, however, take us to a subject that had never come up in conversation, police records, or the trial — drugs. For some time after the murders, I and others close to the situation were routinely asked if the killers were high on drugs, or more accurately, in a drug-induced blood lust. The question was a natural, given the striking savagery of the attacks and the absence of any explanation for it. For most people, it was simply a given. My answer has always been no. But when Karen and I asked about drugs, Milton volunteered that they could have been drinking or using something inasmuch as they often did drink and sometimes got high on other things (not specified). In my thinking, the drug/alcohol factor has always been a non-issue. As a potentially mitigating circumstance, they or their counsel would have brought it up. Nowhere in the statements to police or the weeks of testimony and motions for both trials were the words even mentioned. While Milton's recent comments to us do raise the question, I'm still inclined to think it was a minor factor. Documented events of both nights reveal two people carrying out a planned attack that involved preparation, teamwork, and scripted deception. Had they been drinking or smoking beforehand? Quite possibly, but they were in complete control of their faculties. Moreover, had it been a central feature of the crimes, especially as an exculpatory condition, somewhere it would have come up and Milton would not have mentioned it 17 years later as just a probability about which he was uncertain. Certainly any mind-altering substance can affect judgment, even in small amounts, but these were singularly vicious assaults that, if attributable to drugs or alcohol, would have required, in my view, a level precluding the systematic execution of their plans.

Our conversation continued to various other subjects but always revolved around or returned to the reason we were there and Milton was there. During one of these discussions, Milton looked directly at me, as he had 12 years earlier, and apologized. In the same words as the first time he said, "I'm sorry about your brother," and then turned to Karen and added, "... and your friend." Karen and I both commented later on his sensitivity in acknowledging her loss as well as mine and also what it said about his lucidity. This was a different person from the man in the letter. Naturally enough, the apology elicited the issue of his crime and culpability. In that context he said at one point, "My mother says Jesus forgives me." That may have been a cue for me to offer forgiveness, but I simply told him he should believe his mother. Karen nodded in assent. It seemed he took considerable comfort in our reactions. And I have no reservations about my response and I'm thankful I was not asked about my own forgiveness. I'm not sure I could ever forgive him, but I do believe he is sincerely contrite and has paid the price for his crime. For those who so lamented the absence of the death penalty at the time, this may sound soft-headed and perhaps is. But if the name "Correctional Facility" as distinguished from, say, "Retribution Center" has any meaning, I'd probably support his release were it possible. My vote for his eventual parole would have to come from beyond the grave. For now, I'll vote with his mother.

An unexpected expansion on the subject occurred after we thought the visit was over. Karen and I were about to leave the room when we were stopped by the "count." Several times a day, all prisoners are counted and during that time everyone is frozen in place. So we returned to the table and sat down again. The circumstances lent the expected superficiality to the conversation but suddenly, Milton looked at me and asked, "Do it hurt you to see me?" It was spoken in his street patois and reminded me of his description years ago of his interrogation by the police: "They had me all skeered up." Still, the question caught me off guard, so perhaps I was temporizing when I responded with my own question: "What do you think?" He guessed it probably did, and I told him that he was right but that it was easier than in the first couple visits. Then, in sharp contrast to his choice of words a minute earlier, he nodded and recalled how the first visit, especially, had been "awkward."

"All skeered up" poses a question I doubt will be resolved entirely. That comment made first to Ann and me in 1992 alluded to his contention of having been bullied into the confessions he made to the police. At that time I was neither surprised nor concerned. Indeed, throughout the trial, each time a legality threatened to quash evidence or testimony, I marveled at how easily they both might have gone free or pled to a far lesser crime had they known not to incriminate themselves. The police knew it too. I doubt that either Milton or Teddy seriously expects to ever be exonerated, but 20 years after the crime, Milton still remembered vividly being intimidated and tricked by his captors. It first came up in the "all skeered up" remark, but his outrage persists to this day. He does not allege innocence, but is unwavering in his insistence that what he said to police was extracted by deception.

Following the May 2004 visit to Wende, I received a letter, this time relatively brief and pointed. Providing an insight into his personality, he begins by reasserting the injustice of his punishment combined with an explanation of why he hadn't brought this up during our visit. This statement is jarring, particularly after

I had become accustomed to speed-reading his letters because of the voluminous scripture quotations and allusions.

"I don't like to argue so I'm writing this in my letter to you. What I did to your brother would not have resulted in his death had that been the only thing done." He then alleges that he was "ordered" to sign a document that was represented to him as verification that he had been told his rights. What he signed instead was a waiver of his Miranda rights. When he realized the deception, he appealed to detectives Lonergan, Frank, and Zientek, insisting that he was not a murderer. Their response was to scream and pound the desk so that they "... made me believe they were going to shoot me dead." Milton's next line reads, "Well I'm going to go now, I'll talk to you later." Following that is a verbatim quotation of the parable of the Pharisee and tax collector.

Is it plausible that, under the circumstances, his version of a 17-year-old street kid being duped into confessing to more than he really did is accurate? Surely it is, but I doubt that Milton understands that, had his participation been limited to waiting on the steps throughout, his penalty would have not changed once convicted of felony murder. It seems he needs someone to believe that he is not a cold-blooded killer. He may not be now, but probably was for just too long. The paradox of two gentle giants possessing a trait sharply inconsistent with gentleness remains and grows. The puzzle becomes almost surreal in the words of Milton's Christmas card from 1999:

Dear Ray,

I'm sending this card to you, Ann, Joanne, Paul, Cheryl, Marya, Keith, Matthew, and Brian, along with the rest of the family because I know that Joe would have sent you all a Christmas card among other things. Remember that people you miss the most are always alive in your heart.

Happy New Year!

Sincerely Yours,

Milton Jones

88-B-2329